ROW AL

Rowing an Ocean to save our Oceans and inspire others

Written and self-published by Dawn Wood

First edition

ISBN: 9781099377358

"For everyone who has supported me in any way big or small, you are all a part of this journey."

"This book is especially dedicated to my wonderful parents Barry and Sheila Smith who worked tirelessly at spreading awareness of my campaign, arranging the amazing welcome into Barbados and generally just being incredibly supportive. I could not have done it without you."

"I cannot have a dedication section without thanking Jaime Wood my husband, he has supported me during the whole campaign despite it taking up a huge amount of our time together.

I love you"

Picture by Becky Plummer (Thank you Becky)

"If everyone makes a small change, together we can make a massive difference"

Dawn Wood

Contents

Foreword

A little note before I begin

I have written this book due to a huge number of requests for me to publish my ocean blogs. I absolutely cannot believe the number of supporters and followers I have had; I did not expect to have such a massive impact on people. I have been overwhelmed with the messages, comments and kind donations. There are so many people to thank, I may have rowed solo, but the adventure has been a team effort. I could not have done this without the support of friends, family and people I have never even met. You have all been amazing and truly are a part of the Row Aurora story.

This book outlines my life leading up to the row and explains how I came to be sitting in a tiny boat in the middle of the ocean, my daily blogs whilst at sea and the whirlwind I experienced after touching land (and still am).

Aims

The aims and objectives of my campaign

When starting out on this mission I set myself goals. The only one I did not fulfil was to beat the world record.

I was of course disappointed, but after reading this book I hope you will agree that all the positive aspects of this campaign outweigh missing the record.

I have used this as a positive part of my talks in schools. It shows that you can dare to dream big knowing that the journey is sometimes more important than the goal. Not one person I have spoken to thinks I have failed even though at times I was scared I had let everyone down, including myself.

- To row 3000 miles across the Atlantic Ocean - solo and un-supported.
- To break the world record for the fastest time a solo female has crossed the Atlantic. Currently set at 49 days.
- To become only the 7th woman in the world to have completed this challenge.
- Raise £20,000 for the Marine Conservation Society.
- Encourage others to reduce their single use plastics.
- Collect evidence of ocean pollution to be used in essential research.
- To inspire others to challenge themselves

Where it began

The start of the adventure

Don't worry, I am not going to bore you with my entire life story, I will just pick out the best and most relevant bits. I am sure you all want to get to the exciting bit hearing about my Atlantic row, but I thought it would be nice to tell you a bit more about me and how I came to choose such a massive challenge.

I was born during the hottest summer on record at that time in 1976 to Barry and Sheila Smith in Barking hospital. My mum tells a funny story about how the nurse came in asking if she wanted an electric fan, to which my dad replied "yes please, I am sweltering" thinking the nurse was talking to him and then proceeded to sit there with the fan pointing at him.

We lived in Upton Park in London with my Nan (Dad's mum) Rose Smith. Four years after I was born, my little brother Gary came along, he is now a 6ft 3 firefighter, but I still call him 'little bruv!!' My Dad was a firefighter, mum a nurse and as you will hear I later went on to join the Police so quite the emergency service family.

We all moved to South Woodham Ferrers in Essex when I was eight years old, where my brother and I had a great time growing up. I am sure my brother has some stories to tell about me picking on him that may change your opinion of me, but I can't see what's wrong with making your sibling eat 24 packs of crisps in one sitting so you can get the free gift promotion!!! I hope my brother never writes a book as that is one of the nicer stories, he will have to tell about me.

When I turned 13, I joined 2531 Squadron of the Air Training Corps, this was the start of my love of adventure. The ATC's motto is 'Venture Adventure' me and many of my friends from those days have lived by this ever since. We used to go flying and gliding on a regular basis, shooting, physical training and Duke of Edinburgh awards expeditions amongst other adventure training. The group of friends I made there are all still in touch and they all clubbed together to sponsor my row as 'THE 2531 GANG' as we are now known.

In those days there were far fewer health and safety worries, I would regularly come home covered head to foot in mud where we had run through the river bank when the tide was out or crawled through a rancid ditch pretending we were evading capture from some enemy forces. Needless to say, I had strict instructions to go straight through the back gate when I got home into the garden where I would be hosed down before being allowed in the house. Ahhhh, happy times!!

I stayed in the air cadets from 1989 until 1997 where I reached the rank of CWO (Cadet Warrant Officer). These were absolutely some of the best days of my life and I met people that are still amazing friends today.

These times were also where I had my first experience of the water which is now my passion. My friend Nicola's parents were keen sailors and Nic herself had her own little mirror dinghy. One day we decided to take the dinghy out for a sail, I am pretty sure this was my first adventure on a boat. Off we went, again with health and safety a concept not part of our vocabulary, launched this little boat and in we got. I had zero idea of what I was supposed to do but how hard can it be? Now, before I get to the punchline of this story, I need to explain something I know now but did not know then... ropes on boats are called sheets. For example, the rope that controls the main sail is called the mainsheet. So off we went pulling 'ropes' and getting up quite a speed, in fact the wind picked up and we were now doing what felt like 20kts directly towards the bank, I was getting pretty scared. A man was standing on the sea wall watching the madness unfold, he was obviously a sailor himself and realised we needed to pull in the sail so began shouting "Sheet in…. Sheet in!!!" I assumed this was an observation of what I was feeling at the time and responded "Yes your right… I am sheeting it; I am really scared"

We managed to get full control of the boat without any damage to us or the boat, which of course made this a very successful first experience at sea and the first steppingstone to my career as a commercial mariner. What could possibly go wrong with such a successful introduction to the water?

My first crossing of the English Channel was also with Nic and her parents Conrad and Heather. We sailed from Tollesbury in Essex across the channel to Belgium down the coast and back to the UK from France. I absolutely loved this experience and my heart was set on a life on the water, however, I did not really get to develop my skills for another few years to come.

Life after school

The big wide world

I left school after completing 6th form with some reasonable but not outstanding results. This is one of the messages I want to give to people, but, young people, I was never a natural athlete or academic. In fact, I was usually the slightly overweight kid who got picked for sports day only if half the school was off with salmonella poisoning (salmonella was quite popular in the 1980's!!). My GCSE and A level results were also not terrible, but I was never good enough at any subject to get A's in anything. My best results were in Art and P.E, I knew from this I would go on to do something in a practical or creative field, I was never going to be in a job sitting in an office. Yet here I am today writing a book after rowing 3000miles across the Atlantic Ocean.

I truly believe that everyone no matter where they are from, what their abilities or disabilities are or what their background is, they have something in them that they can excel in and inspire others to do the same. If you don't reach your goal, find a new route to get there or don't be afraid to choose a new goal. Better to reach for the stars and miss than reach the gutter and find it. I got that saying from Matt who I became friends with at air cadets, he went on to be an RAF jet pilot!!! So, these are not just fancy words that I have made into a saying, they are words that have molded the future of many inspiring men and women.

With my ok, but not outstanding results the time had come to earn my keep and find a job. My dream was to follow in my dad's footsteps and become a firefighter. I had done a period of work experience at the Essex Fire and Rescue Service HQ whilst at school, I absolutely loved it and I even remember being interviewed for a newspaper article where I declared I would become the first female chief officer in ECFRS (Essex County Fire and Rescue Service). I took part in (Pre H+S) drills in the smoke chamber wearing breathing apparatus with zero visibility and even rode in the fire appliance to a 'shout' when a live job came in. I felt totally at home here, looking back on it, a 15-year-old girl in a male dominated environment I should have been like a fish out of water, but it was so natural for me to be there.

I never did get to join the fire service as at the time I applied (1994 I think) there was a height restriction of 5ft 6 and I am only 5ft 5, so I never did become the first female senior officer. Did I fail? Absolutely not!! For a 15 year old chubby girl with average GCSE results to declare she was going to succeed in an environment where no female had ever gone before was an incredible goal to aim for, something beyond my control meant I could not achieve it so rather than give up, I simply diverted my path and goal slightly.

As I write this it reminds me of a story I heard from very recently from an inspirational speaker, Paula Craig MBE. She was a marathon runner, again not a natural athlete, but due to hard work and dedication started to achieve sub 3hr marathon times. Whilst out training on her bike for a triathlon she was involved in an accident leaving her paralysed from the waist down. When the rehabilitation team asked her what her goals were she replied "enter the London marathon as a wheelchair athlete" they replied "Oh, that's great, but we was thinking of something like learn to put your socks on for yourself" Clearly the obstacles I have had to overcome are nothing compared to this, but I just love that fact that this lady did not set her goal to what society may have expected her to but where she believed they should be. She did in fact go on to become the first athlete to enter the London marathon as both a runner and wheelchair athlete.

With my fire service application rejected and 6th form finished I needed to find a job, there was no way I was going to sit on my behind expecting anyone else to look after me. I still lived at home with my parents and 'little bruv' I am sure they would have looked after me if needed, but I had been brought up to take responsibility for myself and have a sense of pride for my own future. My friend from school Mel, who again I am still amazing friends with now, was very good at the sciences and had a job in a laboratory. I had done A-level chemistry with her, she got a very good result, and I got ungraded. Before our A-level results came through she bigged me up to the boss and I got an interview for a job in her lab. This lab was testing malt for making beer at a malting's company in Witham, Essex. Luckily my interviewing skills must have shone thorough as I got the job and never had to declare I failed A level chemistry!

I was never going to make this my career, but I would not change a single day of working there. I met some amazing people and learnt so many life skills. Mel, of course, I already knew; then there was, Jean, Sally, Kim, Karen, James, Sue, Carole and all the guys in the factory and offices. Who remembers all the people they worked with 25 years ago?? I do which is a testament to the impact they had on my life. We worked hard but also had some incredible laughs.

After a couple of years working in a laboratory, I was accepted into Essex Police. I joined the ranks on the 6th of June 1996. My original posting was to Southend a seaside town in Essex, some of the best days of my career were had here with some of the best old school officers I have ever met. I did 3 years 'on the beat' followed by 3 years on a proactive team dealing with drugs and vice. As a 21-year-old who looked much younger than I was, I was often used as a decoy in school uniform to catch the local flasher and catch curb crawlers who were after young girls. I have some funny stories about these days, but this book is about my Atlantic row and how I got there so don't want to take too much time up here. However, I will give you one story.

We were working in an area of Southend where prostitution was a problem it was 1999. My personal view on this matter is that is that, although I would never choose this as a career path of my own, if there are people willing to work in this industry and people willing to pay, why not make it legal and keep it in a safe environment for everyone? As it was, the 'ladies' were working in a residential area meaning curb crawlers were causing distress to women (well everyone actually) who lived there. This was not acceptable, and our pro-active team decided to act. I was hidden in the boot of an old Ford Escort whilst my mate (appropriate and real name) Tommy, drove the car looking for ladies of the night to educate. The idea was that a prostitute would get in the car and once she had said enough to secure a prosecution, I would push the back seat down and jump out of the boot to make the arrest.

I heard the car pull over and Tommy say, "hi there, what are you doing here?" a woman's voice replied "Anything you want baby" I heard her get in the car and the door close. There was no real conversation that followed, it was more of a menu/ price list being read out for services that at my young age did not really know what on earth were. I was no innocent wall flower, but this woman clearly had skills I had never even heard of!! Through the small gap in the rear seat I could now see that she was also 'giving a display' of what was on offer!! Tommy looked distraught, despite being ten years older than me he was also a lot more innocent.

I realised the time had come to reveal we were old bill and secure evidence for prosecution. I pushed on the back of the seat only to find it had locked back and I was now trapped in the boot. I started to struggle with the seat trying desperately to get out before Tommy was the victim of an assault that he did not even know the description of. The lady passenger now heard my struggle and herself started to panic wondering why this man had a woman trapped in the boot. Tommy automatically locked the doors to prevent her escape from police custody, however in the confusion she thought she was being held prisoner to join me the boot of this serial killer's car. There was a very tense few minutes that followed with her trying to defend herself from a serial killer's car and trying to rescue me from his murderous plans.

Eventually I managed to get out and embraced this woman, firstly to thank her for her rescue efforts and secondly to reassure her that she was not the victim of the modern-day Jack the Ripper. Once everyone had calmed down and had a full understanding of what had actually happened, we let the woman go on her way without being reported or risk of prosecution. I think she was probably put off more from this experience than any court could have done.

I then passed my firearms course in 2002 and worked for a period at Stansted Airport as an authorised firearms officer before finally moving to the marine section in 2004. As I had come from an armed role at Stansted Airport, I kept my firearms permit in date by attending regular training and attachments with the armed response teams and force support unit. I took part in several maritime firearms jobs including the first maritime Taser deployment in the UK. After 9 years on the marine section and achieving my Yachtmaster qualification as well as instructor status in many maritime disciplines, I was offered the opportunity to become a firearms instructor.

In 2013 I became a firearms instructor making this my main role but keeping up my maritime skills by being a marine unit officer on a part time basis. I loved these years as it was such a rewarding job, to see someone who had never held a gun in their life to someone who could perform the role of an authorised firearms officer was incredible. I have so many stories about these days, but maybe I will write another book about my police days. This book is about my Atlantic adventures and how I got there.

In April 2017 I applied for a full-time role back with the marine section. I loved working in the tactical firearms environment, but my absolute passion was on the water so this was an opportunity that I could not turn down. Since then I have continued to develop my maritime skills both at work and in my spare time. I am now a commercially endorsed Yachtmaster instructor and the principle for the marine unit sea school.

Marine Section

My day job

I have told you a little bit about my role on the Essex Police Marine Section but as it's such an unusual role I thought I would give you a bit more information. As a unit we patrol approximately 400 miles of coastline from the Dartford River crossing to Mistley (Near Harwich) We have one large patrol vessel Alert IV and a smaller but faster RhIB (Rigid hulled inflatable boat) We cover a whole host of incidents from working with UK Boarder Force and other agencies to public reassurance at high profile events. During heightened security states in the past we have conducted 24hr armed patrols and at all states of security we have a role in protecting our vulnerable sites across the coastline.

Over the years I have also had to sadly recover many dead bodies not only from our coastline but from inland lakes rivers and ponds. This is one of the sad parts of my job as we often have the task of also informing the family. I have recovered people who have taken their own life, been involved in an accident or incident at sea or on occasions have been the victim of a murder. The ones that have the most effect on me are the children, I still remember clear as if it were yesterday searching an area of coastline for a missing child all through the night. The little girl's family could be heard calling her name all night along the beach. Her body was recovered the following day. I am also swift water rescue trained so will often get called out to search for missing people or property in fast flowing water.

A few years ago, we had quite substantial flooding in Essex, me and my team spent the whole night rescuing people from their cars trapped in flood water. I had to pull the passenger from one car after the driver had come off the road into a ditch. The road was 3 foot deep in flood water so the edge of the road could not be seen. Once the car was in the ditch it began sinking, the driver managed to get out, but the passenger was disabled so was not able to get out. I had to swim out, force the door open against the force of the water then carry the man to safety. That was a pretty eventful night, what got me about that night is we never got any thanks, the only comments we got were from drivers who shouted at us annoyed that they could not get down the road we had just blocked off for their own safety. There is obviously a good side to the job too. I have worked really hard to work my way up to become a commercially endorsed Yachtmaster and Yachtmaster instructor, these are internationally recognised qualifications, so I am really grateful to have had the opportunity to achieve this as part of my role. I have led raids on ships believed to be involved in terrorism, conducted surveillance operations at night and generally got to get involved in some 'James Bond' style operations. Better a bad day on the water than a good day in the office I always say!!

Me and Sports

Keeping fit

Over the years I have taken part in many sports, usually ones which involve coming home with bruises!! I played hockey for my local team and represented Essex Police. My favorite position was in goal because I was not so good on the pitch. I seemed to have a natural talent for goal keeping, plus I was the only one on the pitch who got to wear a helmet and full set of pads, not as stupid as I look!!

Rugby has been one of my passions, I have not played for about six years and I do miss it, but I think I enjoy watching more than playing now. I played for my local team in Burnham and for the mighty Blue Birds at Chelmsford Rugby Club, the Blue Birds are still going strong with a pretty high standard of rugby. Chelmsford Rugby Club were kind enough to sponsor my row and I was proud to display their logo on my boat. I also represented British Police many years ago, but this is a distant memory now. You would not think it to look at me now, but I played prop on occasions, but my regular position was hooker or flanker. I am starting to change my mind about enjoying watching more than playing as I type this, should I dust off my boots and come out of retirement?? Scuba diving is something I really love; I am an advanced diver but I have not done it for so long that I would need to do a refresher course now. During the coming months I intend to do something about this and get back into it. I took up running about 15 years ago to lose weight, but I have got to be honest I don't really enjoy it which is why I never really stuck to it. At work I must pass a fitness test every year, during the time I was a firearm's officer I had to achieve quite a high standard. Well, it's a high standard to me as I am not naturally athletic so had to work really hard to reach the fitness level required. You could tell when it was fitness test time as I would be out running every day and be about a UK size 10-12, once the test was passed, I would stop running and gradually get bigger and bigger. Then a couple of months before fitness testing came around the whole process started again. Now I have discovered rowing and weight training as a way of keeping fit, I absolutely love both sports so it's easy to keep it going and not get back into the cycle of periods of no exercise at all. If you see me out running today, I would join in if I were you as I will be doing it to escape some sort of zombie apocalypse and not for fun.

Getting involved in rowing

One oar or two

In 2014 I had one of my first rowing experiences in a wooden gig as part of the Harkers yard rowing series for Burnham on Crouch Coastal Rowing Club. All the boats rowing in the Harkers yard races are identical and made by Pioneer Trust which is a charitable organisation. They teach boat building skills to young people as one of its aims amongst lots of other valuable goals. The boats are fixed seat with four rowers and a coxswain, they are very different to the ocean rowing boat I have just crossed the Atlantic in.

I received a call from my friend Jerry who said they had a rowing race at the weekend, and would I fancy taking part. I had a huge amount of maritime experience and could skipper a Police launch like a demon, however, rowing was not something I had a lot of experience in. How hard could it be? So along I went and was literally thrown in at the deep end!! The races were only about 2 miles long, but you need a huge amount of strength and cardio fitness to get the boat moving. The boats are traditional design, so the oars are solid wood and much heavier than modern carbon fiber ones. I am pretty sure we came last in that race, but from that moment I was hooked!!

I quickly progressed through the club from ladies captain and then on to club Chairman, a role I still hold today. The president of the rowing club is Charlie Pitcher, this is where the Ocean rowing link comes in. Charlie holds several ocean rowing world records himself and is the founder of Rannoch Adventure. Rannoch is a company dedicated to supporting Ocean rowers including the design and supply of the boats themselves. They are based in Burnham-on-Crouch just a few miles away from where I live so it was almost inevitable that this was going to happen.

Charlie knew about my passion for rowing and the water, but when he heard about my qualifications to teach all sorts of maritime subjects such as navigation, first aid and seamanship, he asked me to help with a project he was running in China.

Shantou University in China wanted to run an expedition along the coast of China into Hong Kong, this was a 300-mile route and there were to be two 5 person Ocean rowing boats taking part. With hundreds of applicants, as well as training them, we had to choose the final crews to take part by setting assessed tasks and fitness testing. Initially my role was to teach navigation and seamanship, but as the project progressed, I ended up learning more about the ocean rowing boats and taking the students out on the open water myself. The final expedition was a massive success and I took part as a safety boat driver.

At the end of the project four of the girls went on to row the Atlantic themselves as a team of four, I was incredibly proud of them and stayed up to watch their live video as they arrived in Antigua. However, I now realised that I could not tell people I helped to train them but not actually do it myself. I knew at this point I was going to row an ocean, I just did not know when, how or who with.

There always seemed to be a reason for me not to do it, not enough time to train, too busy to take three months out, not enough money, not fit enough etc etc. There were so many reasons I kept on telling myself not to do it, although it was my dream I think deep down I was scared of failing so it was easier to find excuses not to do it rather than admit I was worried about failure.

In April 2018 I went to the Rannoch Ocean rowing open day to have a general chat with everyone there and get some more information. Although I was already ten times more qualified and knowledgeable than I needed to be, I really do like to make sure I know my subject inside and out and I never leave anything to chance where the ocean is concerned. I plan for everything!! Whist there I spoke with Kiko Matthews who had just returned from her own solo ocean row and proud owner of the world record. I listened to her speak and realised that if she could do it then so could I, the things she was saying basically blew my arguments of why I hadn't committed to do it. I knew from that point I was going to row an ocean solo, I just needed to get the ball rolling.

Conservation

Our planet

As you have probably worked out by now, I absolutely love the water it's my passion and I get withdrawal symptoms if I am away from it too long. However, being on the water almost every day of my life means I have witnessed so much of the pollution and rubbish we throw into our waters and seen the damage it causes. Every day I am out I collect rubbish, a lot of rubbish!!

The main offenders are balloons, its unusual not to pick up a balloon every time I go out on the water. Next, plastic bottles and bags and during the summer I collect between 30-40 beach toys per weekend that have blown off our seaside areas.

A few years ago, I volunteered for a marine mammal rescue charity and got involved in a few seal rescues. I also got involved with an international exchange dealing with marine pollution from commercial shipping.

As I said I always collect any rubbish I come across whist on the water, but I wanted to do more to help. When I made the decision to take on the Atlantic solo I realised I could use this to raise awareness about the problem and encourage others to reduce their single use plastic consumption. I never imagined the impact I would have when I started, I thought maybe a few people might stop using straws or something. But the response has been beyond belief. I often talk in schools, and whenever I do, I always receive a whole load of messages telling me how their son or daughter has started collecting rubbish to and from school, or has started using a reusable drinks bottle rather than a single use plastic one. I have received messages from schools across the world with photographs of the projects they are doing dedicated to me. It's not just the children, lots of adults have messaged me to tell me how they have changed their plastic habits, and it's made the whole thing worthwhile to hear the number of people who have made a change.

Moving forward I am not going to stop the ball from rolling now. I have lots of plans for events and initiatives and of course there will eventually be another big challenge. As I write this I am not sure yet what that will be, but as you read I may have already announced or even done it.

Taking the first step

The hard work begins

On the Monday after the ocean rowing open day I went into Rannoch adventure to discuss my plan. I also needed to see what boats they had for sale and book them to help me with my training, weather routing, shore support and shipping. Rowing an ocean is not just about getting in the boat and rowing, the months that followed this moment was constant stream of training, planning, admin and hard work. Once I had declared my commitment, the ball started rolling and the sleepless nights began. There were plenty of times I prayed for the day to come where I would be on my own with the ocean and no contact with the outside world as I was suddenly in a situation where I had zero time for myself to relax or just do normal day to day tasks. There was constantly a job to do or an email to send it became a second job, I was exhausted.

The first job was to find a boat. As I was doing this to raise awareness about plastic pollution, I decided to go for a secondhand boat rather than commission a new one. Calling it second hand does not do it justice!! I feel like people expect to see a battered old thing with 'one careful owner' sticker on the side. In fact, my boat 'True Blue' had two careful owners both of whom had crossed the Atlantic successfully and safely. True Blue is a 'Rannoch' purpose-built ocean rowing boat model R10. This is a 21ft one-person rowing boat built to self-right should it capsize. The sister ship of True Blue is called 'SOMA OF ESSEX' and is said to be "The fastest and safest ocean rowing boat ever built".

True Blue is fitted with equipment such as water maker, navigation plotter, radios, emergency safety equipment and positioning beacons all of which I need to ensure I am fully trained in. All equipment on board is powered by solar panels which I also need to ensure I know to fix in the event of a power failure. I will explain more about this training later in this book.

I was very excited to meet True Blue but at a cost of £46,000 I was about to commit myself to a massive task of fundraising. Could I do it? Was I really up to the task? Will I be able to get sponsors? Will people take me seriously? A thousand questions were going through my head. This boat cost more money that my first house, what on earth was I doing?? I did not only need to find the money for the boat, there was also shipping £10K equipment £6K, food £1.5K, training courses, medical equipment, flights, accommodation and the list goes on. I also wanted to raise money for the Marine Conservation Society on top of all this. Sitting looking at the figures gave me nightmares. I had just 8 months before I would be flying out to Gran Canaria for the start of my row.

I knew it was a risk, but I was not the first person to do this so if they could do it why couldn't I? So, the handshake was made and with a personal bank account consisting of -£1,547.55 I now had the monumental task of raising enough money to not only row across the Atlantic Solo and unsupported, but also donating a significant amount to my chosen charity.

I put down a £6,000 deposit which I got from my first sponsor, Station Automotive, they could not really say no and it was a dead cert as this is my husband Jaimie's business. We have been married since March 2015 and he supports everything I do. The people who have asked him why he 'allowed' me to do this row always get the same reply, "If I had said no, she would have done it anyway, it's about supporting each other in achieving our dreams"

The next big chunk of the money came from bank loans. I borrowed £30,000 in total, the repayments were pretty high so we would be eating budget beans on toast for a while, but it took a huge amount of pressure off. I had a lot less money to raise from sponsors and the whole task became less daunting.

Setting up the campaign

Learning new skills

I had now secured a boat which I was due to collect at the end of May 2018. I had the goal which was to row 3000miles across the Atlantic Ocean Solo and unsupported. I had the cause to raise awareness about plastic pollution in our oceans and encourage others to reduce their single use plastic, but I still needed to raise the rest of the money. To do this I was going to need to set up my campaign starting with a website.

I went online and taught myself how to set up my own website, with very little experience in this and very bad IT skills this was not easy. I quickly realised that I now had created myself a spider's web of extra jobs. My website needed a logo, I would have to set up a charitable organisation bank account, I would need to start book keeping my spending and income, I needed professional photos for the website, I needed media coverage to show my site was credible, information brochure for potential sponsors, campaign name, aims and goals for the campaign, social media accounts. The list of tasks just trying to set up a website created was mind blowing!! I started writing a list of all the jobs that needed doing and put them in order of importance before picking them off one by one.

Job one, name the campaign. You may have wondered why I called my campaign Row Aurora? Well you are about to find out. I thought long and hard about this, if it was not right at the point I announced it, it would be too late. It had to be right from the start. It needed to sound professional so that potential sponsors would take me seriously, it needed to be relevant to me, it needed to be catchy and not cheesy and I had to make sure nobody else was using the title. I toyed with lots of ideas 'Dawn of the Row' 'OarWood' 'Dawn of the Ocean' and many more. I decided to contemplate my campaign name over a pint in our local pub when I saw a plaque from warship 'HMS Aurora'. Aurora is Latin for Dawn and is the symbol for new beginnings as in the sunrise. This was perfect, I loved it, 'Row Aurora' was born. I then needed to register my website www.rowaurora.co.uk The domain was not being used so I set to work putting the site together. It was not the most professional site, but it was pretty amazing considering I had very little experience or content to add to it.

Next was the logo, I came up with a rough version of what I wanted it to look like and contacted my friend Paul Leister who use to design logos as a business. Once I told him what I was doing he was incredibly supportive and got to work almost immediately. Within a couple of weeks I now had a professional logo to add to my site and any promotional material.

Getting sponsors

Or not!!!

Although I had self-funded a huge part of this campaign, I still needed help to make it happen. With my credit cards maxed out and not enough income to make repayments of anymore loans I had to start asking sponsors to get on board. This is not as easy task as you would think, you don't just give Richard Branson a bell and get a cheque five minutes later, its HARD work. Firstly I had to put a professional brochure together outlining what different sponsorship options would cost and what they would get in return, this had to be short enough that readers would not get bored but also have enough information to put across my cause and why it would be of benefit for them to get involved. Sponsors are not going to want their brand linked with something that is unprofessional or has no credibility.

Putting the brochure together was a tough task and there were several versions before I was ready to start sending it out. The clock was ticking!!! Over the coming months I dread to think the number of emails and letters I sent out and the hours of time spent at my computer researching the best person to contact from my chosen companies who I was sure would love to sponsor me. I quickly learnt that unless you had a personal contact in most of these corporations your email or letter would probably never get read and more than likely deleted. It was extremely demoralising, I was working so hard to make this happen, but I just don't know anyone rich or famous to help my campaign gain momentum or credibility.

I had gone too far to give up, but I had some sleepless nights trying to work out how this was ever going to happen. The few replies I did get wished me well in my mission but explained that they had already allocated money to their chosen charity for that year. I was beginning to think I had made the biggest mistake of my life. I could not let these negative thoughts get out publicly, I had to show the world I was ready for action and everything was on track. If I gave away the fact I thought the future of my campaign was doomed then how could I expect everyone else to believe in me. I had to try another tack.

Next, I launched the 250 club where people could have their name on the boat. I loved this as it meant I could take everyone who joined with me in name. At first I was not sure anyone would want to join but I was soon proven wrong. Friends, family and people I had never even met wanted to be part of this incredible journey. I began to realise that this was not going to just be about rowing a boat, it was going to become much more.

Eventually after lots of hard work I started getting contacts from local businesses and friends who wanted their name or business logo on the boat. At the time I was disappointed that I did not have any international companies on board, but now I am so happy that every logo and name mean something special to me. All the business logos are in some way linked to me and have a genuine interest in reducing single use plastics. I will add a list of all my sponsors with an explanation of how we are connected at the end of this book. Although I am going to give them all a special mention, I would really like to tell you about Green Recycling from Maldon.

Rob Smith the director contacted me as he heard about what I was doing via a mutual friend. Green Recycling deals with commercial waste and we had been using them since opening our Garage. Rob offered to become my main sponsor, after visiting the site and listening to him talk I was over the moon to have the company as part of my challenge.

I was shown round the site watching the waste come in, being sorted into different materials by hand then saw where it was bailed up ready for the recycling process. Not one piece of waste ends up in landfill which is an incredible achievement. Now, you would think a recycling company would want us to keep using plastic, so that they could make money out of it. This could not be further from the truth. Low grade single use plastics are of very little value. Countries who use to buy our plastic to recycle have now refused to take any more in, this is because we sent such low grade stuff that there was a huge percentage that was unusable so ended up, guess where, in the Ocean!!

Training

The road to an ocean row is not as easy as you might think. Being able to row is about 10% of the skills needed. I had to make sure I knew the boat inside and out. I left no stone unturned and made sure I was the most prepared person to ever cross an ocean (well in my own head anyway!). I am sure some people thought I was overdoing it but I am programmed to work like this. Every time I identified a risk, I would find a way of reducing it. This meant that I was never scared or worried about anything as I knew I could deal with it.

The first and obvious training was to get my boat 'True Blue' launched and get on the oars. Looking back on the photos she looks very naked without her logos, but she did not stay bare for long. My shift pattern is 6 days (or nights) on duty 3 days off. I was working 9hr shifts, finishing work then rowing for between 4 to 8 hours. My three days off were taken up with longer rows, planning sessions, school talks and other training I had booked in for that week.

It was HARD work. My first three-day row obviously involved staying on the boat overnight. I have many logged night hours at sea, I am no stranger to being out on the water in the hours of darkness and absolutely love the challenge of it. However, all my experience is on board a boat with crew and engines!! Being on my own at night in a tiny rowing boat whilst facing the wrong way was a whole different ball game. One of the big issues is collision avoidance. During the day it's much easier to see other vessels and for them to see me, it's also easier to work out the direction they are travelling and how to avoid a collision. At night it's much harder.

Lights on boats are sectored, which means you will see different coloured lights depending on the aspect you are viewing it from. Being able to work out its aspect will also give you a clue as to what direction it is going in and how to avoid it.

'True Blue' is fitted with AIS which stands for Automatic Identification System, this will pick up any commercial shipping alerting me to its position and alerting them to my position. It will also pick up any private boats fitted with AIS, but it is not a legal requirement for private boats to have AIS fitted, so night navigation round the Essex coastline is pretty dangerous in a small boat that can do an average speed of 2.5kts.

One of my two-day rows was with my good friend and rowing teammate Kay Tavinor (whose company made my rowing boat!). We set of for a row round into the river Blackwater. I did my usual route planning to work out the tides and which route would be most favourable and off we set. Kay is definitely the girl to take with you on any expedition, she had a full picnic and everything you would expect a fully qualified scout to have in case of emergencies!! If I ever decided to row an Ocean with someone else, she would be the first person I would call. She might not say yes! But she would still be my first port of call.

Although Kay is responsible for building these boats, she had never actually got to row in one. Kay is an extremely experienced sailor and gig rower, so she did not take much time at all getting the hang of everything. However, she suddenly became acutely aware of what a massive task solo rowers take on.

Most of the row so far had been with the wind and or tide, so far so good. The wind was coming from the South West, so we had the wind directly behind us on the way out, as we turned to port (left) and headed up the River Blackwater we had the wind on our port side however, we did now have the incoming tide behind us. We rowed into the early evening before dropping anchor for a couple of hours rest and to wait for the tide to turn. We decided to pick up anchor at midnight and began the row back, this was where the penny dropped, although this was a mere taster, it was a real test of mind over matter. The boat speed against the wind was a very slow and laborious 0.5kts no matter how hard we rowed you just cannot beat nature. To get back down into the river crouch was just 5miles but at half a knot this was going to take ten hours!!!! We started doing two-hour shifts each, which soon went down to one hour, before we got home it went down to 30mins.

This was tough going with two of us, to do this on my own if I had adverse winds in the Atlantic was going to be a real test of character. A tough couple of days on the water, but brilliant training.

The many hours on board True Blue certainly paid off. When I came to do my Atlantic row, my hands were already use to the oars meaning I got no blisters and very few problems. I also knew where every little thing was stored and felt really at home being on board my little ocean home.

More preparation

It's not just about rowing

On top of the on water training I had to learn about the electrics, water maker, weather routing, route planning, logistics into Barbados, logistics out of Gran Canaria, paperwork and documents, ships registration and radio licence this list is not exhaustive. If I did not have the right paperwork, equipment or evidence of qualifications there is the risk that the port authorities would not have let me leave Gran Canaria making the whole thing a disaster. Rannoch Adventure were helping me with elements of this, but as you have probably worked out, I do take a lot of personal responsibility for anything I do. Paying someone else to do my planning and prep and leaving it at that just does not sit well with me.

Rannoch sorted my shipping, which is probably the only thing I had no input in. All I had to do was make sure my boat was packed ready to go the day before shipping safe in the knowledge it would be in port when I arrived in GC. Then all I had to do in Barbados was make sure my boat was clean, tidy and packed, the Rannoch Adventure team would make sure it got to the shipping port and in the container ready for her journey home. As I write this she is still in the container on a ship, I can't wait till she gets home. This was the only element I could not have dealt with on my own, they are the experts, so I entirely left this up to them. Loading, unloading, the lot.

I should introduce you to Angus Collins at this point as he comes up a lot in the rest of the book, he is a true adventurer. Angus has worked for Rannoch Adventure for several years and holds numerous world records for ocean rowing. His passion for the sport is amazing and I really felt I was in good hands with him. I aspire one day to also be able to put my job title as 'Adventurer'.

Angus also helped me with logistics in Gran Canaria, I had done plenty enough prep that had something happened to prevent Angus coming out I could have managed; however, it would have been about 10x harder work. His experience and knowledge is second to none and as you will read later during my weeks prep in GC he was a godsend.

Weather routing was another really important part that I was capable of doing on my own, but if you have ever tried deciphering synoptic charts in 33kts of wind, it's much easier to have someone on shore with access to the internet to give you direction. I spent a lot of time studying trade wind trends and looking at routes to get most benefit from the elements. But the truth is that weather prediction takes a lot of guess work, just ask Michael Fish! (If you are wondering who Michael Fish is, just google him in relation to the storms of 1986, sorry Mr Fish!).

You basically have two choices, do a straight line from A to B or get as far south as you can before going west. Option one is the shortest route (3000 statute miles) but option two is less likely to encounter bad weather and you should pick up the faster trade winds.

The other consideration is that the world is not flat!! This is contrary to some peoples view, but I am very sure the world is round. When you draw a straight line on an admiralty chart this actually becomes a curved line on a gnomonic (globe) chart and is not the shortest route. It takes a bit of explaining here, but if you do an internet search on 'Great circle route' and 'Rhumb line' you will see what I mean. Bet you did not think you would end up doing homework when you bought this book.

The preparation took on the role of a second job and pretty much took over my life. So, at this point I would really like to make a special mention to my friends and family who stood by me.

Whenever I held a fundraising event, they were there selling tickets, decorating venues and generally leading the dancing. When my friends invited me over for an event at theirs, I often turned it down as I had too much to do or was just exhausted, but they continued to support me and I know I have friends for life. Thank you Pammy Marron, Teresa Barr, Jo Bird, Tina Hayden, Brenda Manning, Ali Kirkham and the Rose gang, Toni Johnson, Sarah Guest and the 2531 gang, and the list goes on. Thank you so much.

On the subject of fundraising events, there was a funny moment at my Caribbean night at Burnham Yacht Harbour. I had a great steel band who did a fantastic job, unfortunately I had not told them about the fire system. The smoke machine went on and the alarms went off resulting in the people being ushered out!! Now you would think this would be the end of the night, but this is a Row Aurora party. I started to do an impromptu talk about my boat (I had drunk a few glasses of rum punch, so I am not sure my information was that accurate) which was on display in the car park this was followed up by the steel drums playing outside as Wade (The drummer) had spare drums in the boot of his car. Luckily the party went on into the night even though I did not win the limbo competition.

The final countdown

10, 9, 8, 7........

I continued to work nonstop both at my full-time job as well as planning and prep for my ocean row. On top of this I also managed to fit in a lot of school visits and talks to local groups. I did not think school visits would be a big part of my campaign, but I quickly realised they were so very important. The children were really on board with the message of plastic pollution and I was overwhelmed with the number of messages I received from parents who told me that their child had decided to start a litter pick or reduce their own plastic use by taking reusable drinks bottles to school. As well as the plastic message it was a real humbling experience to have young people approach me and tell me how inspired they were by me. The message I bring to schools is that I was never naturally good at anything at school, I have just worked really hard at anything I put my mind to and generally achieve it. I don't always achieve everything I try either, but I learn from that and use it as a positive to either try a different goal or a new angle to have another go at the original goal. "Better to reach for the starts and miss, than reach for the gutter and find it"

I was also lucky enough to be offered a spot rowing on the royal barge 'Gloriana'. This is the Queens Rowbarge that was built as a lasting legacy to the Queens Diamond Jubilee in 2012. It was a cold and wet day, but a massive honour to row on the iconic River Thames in such an amazing vessel.

As you can see, the lead up to my row was not an easy road, there were times I thought I would never even get to the start line, but the fact I am writing this book tells you I did. I could not have done it without all my amazing sponsors and 250 club members who get a special mention later.

The next part of this book is a record of my blogs written whilst out on the Ocean. Some of these blogs never made it to public domain, so this will be the first time they have been read. I hope you have enjoyed reading so far and further enjoy joining me on my journey which starts with my flight out to Gran Canaria.

28th December 2018

The point of no return

I flew from Stansted Airport to Gran Canaria on the 28th of December waved off by my lovely friends Pammy and Stuart and my wonderful Mum, Dad, brother and if course my husband Jaime who is flying out with me. My Dad made a banner to wave at the airport which was a bit embarrassing as I am quite shy!!!!

Ha ha, only kidding I absolutely loved it. I love how amazing my mum and dad have been. I still have not got emotional as it's not properly sunk in that it's actually happening!! The airport and flight all went without incident which was a surprise! I usually end up dealing with some kind of crisis – I once actually had to deal with a casualty on board a flight as I seemed to be the only one on board who knew first aid. But that's another story!!!

After a bit of trouble trying to find each other, we were collected at the airport in Gran Canaria by Angus Collins from Rannoch Adventure who are helping me get ready in this final week. Angus will also be doing my weather routing but more about that later.

Angus told us that True Blue had been collected from the port and had arrived safe and sound. Slight problem though – all the ports had gone on strike and were not letting anyone in or out!

This was not good news; however, Angus had managed to locate a marina willing to take us which was just 15min drive from Puerto Morgan which was where we were supposed to be.

We drove down to see her and she looked amazing sitting pride of place on the hard. Apparently, the staff at the port had never seen anything quite like it and were very amused about my bucket with a poo symbol on it!!

After giving her the once over it was off to our accommodation. The apartment was nice and clean and a good base for what we needed. The evening was spent doing paperwork and admin, checking everything was in order ready for departure.

29th December 2018

Up an out by 9am today to head down to the marina which is a 15min drive. The day was spent unpacking the entire boat so she was empty and getting rid of a fair bit of kit that I would not need (the chocolate and ginger nut biscuits stayed!!)

It's was amazing to see the amount of kit that came out of my little 21ft boat, a lot of the equipment I will hopefully never need but it would be stupid to go without it. For example, the hand water pump, this is a heavy bit of kit and will probably not need it. But if my main water maker breaks this is essential.

Re-packing everything into the boat also needs careful thinking. If there is too much weight in the stern the boat will drag and slow my progress, too much weight in the bow and the rudder will have less effect making steering a problem. Too much weight on one side and I would have to row hard on the opposite oar to counter steer.

With everything checked off the list and packed back in it was time to go back to the apartment for some weather routing.

The weather at the moment is showing low pressure systems coming across. Low pressure systems move in a counterclockwise direction, so if the bottom of the system is in my way I will end up being blown backwards. Too early to say if this will affect my start date as everything could change over the coming days.

30th December 2018

Getting wet

Today is the day she goes in the water!! and out after a night of broken sleep (our apartment is above a restaurant so can be quite noisy) and down to the marina.

The staff are really helpful and professional and were really interested to know "how it worked" I was asked if there was an engine and where the sails connected! It caused much amusement when I flexed my muscles to show how the boat was being powered.

In she went and I got to row on Atlantic waters for the first time. Ok, it was only within the marina into my berth, but it felt great to be on the oars.

We found the berth and began the task of moving the equipment round to ensure the boat sits perfectly in the water.

There was still a lot of maintenance type jobs to do such as adjust the seat wheels. We had taken the seat back to the apartment yesterday taken all the wheels off and replaced the bearings. The wheels are actually rollerblade wheels but do the job perfectly.

By the time we finished there was only a couple of hours daylight left so we went off shopping. No, we weren't having a couple of hours off. Armed with a list of equipment needed it was off to Decathlon to pick up some final bits needed. For some reason I had packed about 15 head torches, 6 pairs of gloves but only one bottle of sun cream!

This evening's weather routing: The low-pressure systems are still looking problematic, but a 4th Jan start is not ruled out- just need to keep an eye on it.

31st December 2018

New Year's Eve

New Year's Eve on the island is strange, walking round in shorts and t-shirt with Christmas music playing in the shops!

We had to pick up a few more bits this morning from the hardware shop. Sandpaper to smooth the oar handles, multi meter for the tool kit, epoxy for any at-sea repairs, bungee, and spare charging cables.

Armed with the shopping it was back down to the boat with the intention of going out for a training row.

Now the first real problem! The ships GPS has stopped working!!! If this had happened at sea it would not be the end of the world, I have three handheld GPS units on board where I can get my position and paper charts so I can plot my position. As a commercial Yachtmaster and Yachtmaster instructor this is all second nature to me so is certainly nothing to panic about. However, the AIS system runs from the GPS which is one of my safety systems. The AIS allows me to see the position of commercial shipping and for them to see me. It's unlikely I will encounter shipping on my crossing, but in the event I do I really need them to be able to see me.

So, the rest of the day was spent with Angus plugging and unplugging wires and making calls back to Rannoch HQ! We finally got back to the apartment at 7.30pm for some weather routing.

The low-pressure systems seem to be moving further north so if the forecast remains the same then the 4th Jan is looking good. New Year's Eve spent with a takeaway pizza and a bottle of red wine watching the fireworks in London on the TV.

1st January 2019

New Year's Day

Happy New Year everyone! I hope you are enjoying the New Year and have already made a start on those New Year resolutions. Firstly, to cut down on your single use plastics, and secondly to do something that will give you a challenge.

No change of routine today, down to the boat for 10am. However, the amazing news is that the GPS is sorted.

After a lot of fault finding checks and calls to Rannoch HQ in the UK, we managed to track the fault down to a wiring junction which had a small amount of corrosion. The part itself probably cost about 50p!!!! So, although it has taken up a lot of time trying to find the fault, I am taking it all as a positive as I now know what every wire in my boat does and what to check if things go wrong. The wiring has also had a complete going over as it all had to be checked to eventually work out where the fault was.

Weather routing for today: potentially I may be delayed a day to miss the weather system that would bring adverse winds. I will keep you posted, but it is an hour by hour check.

2nd January 2019

Para anchor drills

The winds on the island seem to pick up consistently during the day making for pretty windy afternoons. This is great for my start but not great when you need to get back into the marina after a training row. My boat is pretty light with a high cabin so with strong winds it can be very difficult to manoeuvre. Because of this we made an early start today getting on the water for first light. It was just beautiful watching the sun rise over the marina.

I got my first taste of what it is going to feel like leaving port, it was a strange feeling to think in a few days I would be going out the same route but would not be turning around!!! I did have a chuckle to myself though. Whenever I leave my parents' house I wave for as long as possible out of the car window until I am around the corner and they can no longer see me. I wondered how long my friends waving me off would stand and wave at me, as it will be a good few hours before I am fully out of sight!

Whilst on the water Angus talked me though the Para anchor drills. The Para anchor is basically a parachute under the water attached to 70metres of rope which in turn is connected to the bow (front)- of the boat. I will need to deploy this in the event I have a strong head wind. The anchor fills up from the ocean's current, which will always be going the right direction, and will slow the drift backwards. I hope I never have to use it as its hard work trawling it in and out, plus I will then have piles of wet rope on deck to deal with. This was the first time I had used the para anchor as there is not the space on the River Crouch where I have done most of my training rows from. I am pleased to report the drills went well and (although I hope not to) I am very confident of getting it right out in the ocean.

This afternoon Gary from Rannoch HQ flew in especially to give my wiring the final once over. Rannoch and the team have really gone the extra mile, Gary literally flew in this afternoon, then will fly back tomorrow afternoon!

Weather routing: My predicted start time is now 9am on the 5th of January. The winds are still coming from the south east which means if I leave too early, I would get pushed too far north making my passage more prone to adverse weather systems later down the line. The start location is Puerto Deportivo Pasito Blanco.

3rd January 2019

Auto helm

Another early start today to get out on the water before the wind picks up too much. This morning's drills consisted of auto helm changes. The auto helm is a gadget that connects to the tiller (the bit that you turn to change the position of the rudder) I can set it to steer a course so all I have to do is row and the auto helm will keep the boat pointing the right way. The problem with this bit of kit is that it is constantly working to try and hold a course and the motor can burn out if over used. This means I need to change the auto helm every 4 hours to give it a chance to cool down. I have three auto helms altogether they are called Rodney, Trigger and Del Boy!!!! Play it cool Rodney, play it cool!!!

Lots of messages all day to day I had been on the BBC... again... lol!! I recon I will get the call to go on Strictly next year! Or I'm a Celebrity Get Me Out of Here?

The afternoon was spent fixing some strapping into the boat which will hold everything in place in the event of bad weather. I am very pleased with how it's turned out. The heaviest item on the boat is probably the medical kit, it would be pretty ironic if that fell on my head – so I am pleased it's all strapped in place now.

Weather routing: Still planning for 9am on the 5th although there is potential we may need to push a later start, it really is an hour by hour decision. However, it's unlikely there will ever be a perfect time to leave – it's just a case of picking a good window. I hope it's not delayed too much as Jaime has to fly home on the 5th his flight is 4.30pm.

4th January 2019

It's actually worked quite well that I am not leaving today. It means I now have a day to pick up some last-minute bits I need, get some fresh food in that I can eat in the first few days and do it all without rushing about.

A bit of a lay in, beans on toast for breakfast then out into town to get some shopping.

Walking down the road and who do we see? Friends of ours from Burnham getting out of a cab!!! We knew they were on the island as they are going to be part of the 'when do we stop waving' gang. But to literally bump into them walking down the road was pretty unbelievable. What a lovely surprise.

The rest of the afternoon will be spent catching up on my admin, packing the fresh food and generally tidying up loose ends in the hope I don't come back to lots of work to catch up on.

Weather routing: still looking promising for a 9am start tomorrow. It's going to be a slow hard slog for the first 24hrs but if I can get down south in good time, I should be in a good position to catch the favourable winds.

My next blog will probably be from the ocean!!! I will keep you posted if there are any changes but all being good, this time tomorrow I will be on the oars of an adventure of a lifetime.

5th January 2019

The day is here!!

I managed to get a reasonable night's sleep last night. Off to the marina for 8am to put the last of my kit on board, including fresh bananas and pasta for the first few days.

It was wonderful to be met by lots of smiling faces who had come to wave me off. I gave everyone a hug and said my goodbyes. For me I did not really say a lot! I got in the boat and for the first time started to feel a bit nervous. I was not really sure it was really happening. As Angus untied my lines and pushed me off I whispered to him "oh, I am actually doing this then?!?!" I rowed out of the marina and headed straight onto a course of 200.

I could see Jaime for about half an hour (he didn't wave the whole time) until eventually the features of the land began to disappear.

I had a pretty uneventful day's row, it was quite tough with the wind and waves coming from the east and I kept going for 8hrs solid before stopping for a break.

In 16 years at sea I have never suffered from sea sickness, but I definitely started to feel the effects today. Nothing serious, just a little queasy.

By night fall the island of Gran Canaria was just a silhouette in the distance with a few twinkling lights to light the restaurants on the sea front. I plodded on into the night taking a couple of hours sleep here and there. The night sky was incredible. What a treat! At about 11pm my ship's radio crackled into life with my name "True Blue." it was a sailboat coming from my starboard side. I made contact and once established our courses were safe I continued on into the night.

6th January 2019

First night at sea

I survived my first night at sea. I still don't really feel like eating, so I managed a banana, energy drink and a couple of ginger nut biscuits to keep me going.

At day break I could no longer see land. This is it, I am on my way to Barbados!!! The day saw the wind starting to turn very slightly, this made for a tough row. I was trying to keep a course of 220 degrees. However, my auto helm could not hold the rudder against the wind. This meant I spent most of the day rowing with one oar to hold the boat into the wind. I could not stop rowing or the boat would just blow onto a course of about 280 which was way off. I just had to keep going one handed rowing for about 10hrs just to keep the boat moving in the right direction. If you look on my tracker you can see I was only making about 0.7knots all day! It was hard!

By nightfall the wind had mercy on me. It turned back a little, not a lot, but enough to be able to set my auto helm and set a course while I got a couple of hours well needed sleep!

During the night I made radio contact with a passing ship I picked up on my AIS system. They confirmed that the CPA (closest point of approach) was 1.5miles and wished me a safe passage.

Day 1 0900hrs stats:

Past 24hr Distance 54nm

Total Distance 54nm

Max Speed 2.71kts

Min Speed 2.00kts

Avg Speed 2.25kts

7th January 2019

Still feel a bit fuzzy headed, but much better than yesterday. After a wash and teeth brush it was back to the oars.

Thankfully I am now steering a course of 240 and the wind is more behind me, so it will be a much less stressful day's row. There are some big rolling waves out here, surfs up!! Clocked 11kts down one beast! Look forward to showing you the footage when I get back.

Well, better get back to it.

Hopefully check in again tomorrow.

Day 2 0900hrs stats:

Past 24hr Distance 52nm

Total Distance 106nm

Max Speed 5.45kts

Min Speed 1.62kts

Avg Speed 2.17kts

8th January 2019

A message from Queen Elizabeth

It was blooming freezing by sunset yesterday! Quite a lot of cloud cover plus the waves having an annoying habit of landing on my head, equals a chilly evening. I don't remember reading this in the holiday brochure! I was expecting a day lounging round in a bikini with an evening meal on the aft deck watching the sun set! Instead I am in full waterproofs looking forward to getting into my sleeping bag! Lol!!

My ship's batteries are getting low due to cloud cover so they are not charging as well. I am doing all the right things – turning down the brightness on my screens, turning off anything non-essential and generally managing the power so I can always run my safety equipment.

I have not even listened to any music yet! Just listening to the sound of the ocean! What have I been thinking about? Not a lot really! I have pretty much switched off to the outside world and have been concentrating on my little world here. It's strange, as I look out to the horizon it looks like the earth only stretches out 3miles around me and I am the only one in it. But I have never once felt alone or scared. After all, I can just ring Jaime to pick me up when I have had enough.

This morning, as every morning so far, I stood up to take a look out over the front of the boat. It occurs to me that I will be crossing the Atlantic facing backwards the whole way!!! I can see a ship in the distance... a massive ship! I take a look on my AIS system and see it is the cruise ship Queen Elizabeth.

Radio on……

"Queen Elizabeth, Queen Elizabeth this is True Blue, True Blue-over"

"True Blue this is the Queen Elizabeth- over"

"Good morning sir, I am the rowing vessel about 3 miles off your port side. Can you see me on AIS? I am a solo rower attempting to beat the speed record across the Atlantic, over"

Short pause…..

"True Blue we have you on AIS (laughs) the very best of luck to you ma'am, have a safe passage – over."

"Queen Elizabeth, True Blue. Thank you sir, safe passage to you also – True Blue out"

Perhaps the crew will remember me when I get invited on board by the Queen!!

Day 3 0900hrs stats:

Past 24hr Distance 54nm

Total Distance 160nm

Max Speed 11.22kts

Min Speed 1.08kts

Avg Speed 2.25kts

9th January 2019

A loose knot

Today started rather early with my entire body in the aft locker (the space in the back of the boat which contains the steering and para anchor.)

As reported yesterday, my ship's batteries are lower than I would like due to the cloud coverage. I woke at 2.30am for a rowing shift to discover the port battery at 12.3V (12.2 is the lowest they should be allowed to get). I decided to turn off the auto helm and steer the rest of the hours of darkness to preserve some power.

This involves opening the rear hatch and disconnecting the auto helm. (A pretty straightforward job, just need to time it so a wave does not get in) Then start rowing and adjust the rudder with the steering ropes as needed. I pulled on the starboard (right of the boat) rope and it just kept coming! The knot holding it onto the tiller had come loose and I had just pulled it out through the pulleys. Arhhhh!!!

So in pitch darkness I now had to climb into the locker, find the end of the rope and re feed it through the pulley. I can tell you that the end of the boat is 5ft 5in from the locker opening because that's how tall I am and I was all the way in, just my feet poking out the end!!

Needless to say I managed to reconnect it all and got under way. There is something quite magical about rowing under the stars. The phosphorescence is incredible! It's some kind of plankton which, when disturbed by the oars, glows up bright green. Without any other light pollution around this is quite something to see. I tried to take a photo, but it just comes out black. Might try doing some go pro footage, maybe that will work?

Well, the day is beginning to look a lot more like the holiday brochures I have read! As the sun begins to rise there is not a cloud in the sky, not only will that mean I might be able to take my wet gear off at last, but also get some well needed charge in the batteries.

I am really enjoying rowing today, I am getting used to the waves and how to position my oars depending on the size of the wave and what direction it is coming from. I have a few shin bruises from the first couple of days where the oars hit my leg if I timed it wrong. I am also able to take my waterproofs off making it much easier to row. I still get soaked by the odd rogue wave when least expecting it! But this time the sun quickly dries me out.

Talking about rogue waves! I actually shouted at one earlier... I had one of the deck hatches open to get some food out, a wave caught me unaware and water got in the locker. Fair enough, I am in the ocean! So I waited a couple of hours and the wind seemed to have dropped – so I opened the hatch, bailed it out and made it all nice and dry. At the exact moment I was about to replace the lid, guess what? Another wave right in the locker!!!!! "Were you actually waiting till I finished drying that out?" I shouted? Who to I don't know, but made myself laugh!

Anyway, back to the story. About midday pleased with the amount of sun on the solar panels, I went to check how much charge. 12.8V???? What, that's not good at all. Minimum is 12.2v, max is 14.1. On charge all morning and hardly moved. Slightly concerned I sat back down to row deciding that there must be an obvious explanation! 10-15mins went by whilst I looked at the solar panels directly in front of me on the stern of the boat. Then it hit me... no, not another wave, it was obviously right in front of me!!

My spare oars are tied up one either side of the boat. As the sun rose on my port (left) side it was casting a shadow from the blade of the oar virtually covering the whole panel!!!!! I quickly moved the offending oar to the other side of the boat and hey presto! The meter jumped up 0.1 of a volt almost instantly and has continued to charge nicely all day! Job well done!! Had a brief chat with Charlie from Rannoch HQ via GPS text. The wind is expected to die off later today, this is not a good thing as a bit of wind behind me definitely helps.

I have been on the oars about 8hrs today so far. Am now having a rest before doing the next 4hrs in the tougher conditions. I aim to row 12hrs out of every 24. Before I go, here is a sighting check list....

- Sea turtles- 3
- Dolphins- 0
- Whales- 0 (although heard them in the night)
- Shark- 0
- Floating plastic- 8

Absolutely gutted to have seen more plastic than wildlife. I know the wildlife is out there, I just have not seen it – trouble is that means I have not seen a fraction of the plastic that must also be out here. I am rowing an ocean to try and bring awareness, please spread the word to help reduce single use plastics.

Day 4 0900hrs stats:

Past 24hr Distance 71nm

Total Distance 231nm

Max Speed 7.7kts

Min Speed 0kts

Avg Speed 2.96kts

10th January 2019

Shooting star

Saw the most amazing shooting star last night. It was so bright like a firework, shot straight across the sky in front of me.

Today has brought light winds which are due to be in until Monday. This is not good news as it means much tougher going without a wind behind me.

As the day goes on more and more effort is needed to keep the boat up to speed. It's tough going and the news that it will finish with 'a bit of a head wind' is not what I wanted to hear.

Giving up is not an option! What's the point in doing all this work to get here and just sit round floating in the middle of the Atlantic?

So I got myself together and came up with a new shift system. 2hrs on 15mins off. Then have a 3hr break during the hours of darkness.

So I plodded on beginning to wonder how I was going to keep this up until Monday! I started thinking about my surroundings and began to realise that the sound of the ocean had changed considerably as the day went on. As the wind dropped to nothing there was no sound at all apart from my oars. For the last few days the sound of waves breaking around me had been the normality, now it was silent.

As the sun began to set I knew I had a tough few days ahead with little sleep, but was thankful for: a few days of having a hatch open without worrying it will be filled by a wave at any moment, being able to move about without almost falling over every 5 mins, putting things down on deck and know it won't be soaked 5 mins later.

Day 5 0900hrs stats:

Past 24hr Distance 38nm

Total Distance 269nm

Max Speed 3.25kts

Min Speed 0.54kts

Avg Speed 1.58kts

11th January 2019

Dolphin

2hrs rowing before sunrise after which I had 15mins to get washed changed and ready for the day ahead. What an amazing sunrise, again I was struck by the lack of noise!

Just as I began my second two hour stint of the day I heard the sound of dolphin blowing air from their blow hole. I quickly turned on my go pro- I hope I caught the footage of them, they were stunning going about their business (on their way to work I expect)

For the first time since I have been on the ocean I decided to get some entertainment going to make to hard trudge a little easier. I listened to an audiobook by Freddy Mercury's roadie. It's pretty good.

Another two hours rowing (4 in total) it's 10.30am and time to get the water maker running. This is a pump which sucks up sea water, forces it through a filter and removes the salt so I can drink it. The sound of the pump attracted quite an audience! I heard a tapping sound on the side of the boat, when I looked there was a great big turtle surrounded by fish having a good old nose about the boat. I put my go pro on an extendable rod and tried to get some footage of him under the water.

He went straight to the camera and tried to have a nibble, so I hope I have some great footage of the inside of his mouth! He stayed around for about half an hour before I turned the pump off and got on my way again.

I wondered how old he was and if any other human had ever seen him or was it just me.

I continued the day working 2hrs on 15mins off into the hours of darkness. The sunset shone blues and reds across the flat sea like the colours on an oil slick.

About 11.30pm I spotted a white light, I continued to monitor it and eventually realised the light was getting closer on a constant bearing. I called up the unknown vessel and after some language barrier, established he was a fishing boat and could see me. He even offered me a fish for my voyage!! Mmmm no thanks!

Day 6 0900hrs stats:

Past 24hr Distance 42nm

Total Distance 311nm

Max Speed 4.35kts

Min Speed 1.08kts

Avg Speed 1.75kts

12th January 2019

Rowing through treacle

One week ago today I set out from GC!! It's now 3am and a stiff breeze has set in from the SE this is making my passage even more tough going! I will finish this entry when it's happens.

The rest of today's blog was written a few days later. I feel like I have been dragging the boat through treacle since the 12th January. If I stop rowing I go backwards so every moment on the oars has to count. Anyway…. where were we?

I left you at 3am… it didn't get any easier. The wind had shifted during the night and was now coming from the South South East. This means it was on the port (left) side of the boat trying to push me northwards whereas I needed to go south. It was not a gentle breeze either.

So on the oars it was. I was cold tired and not happy about the whole situation. However, I knew I had to do it as nobody was going to do it for me. Giving up and going to sleep was not an option, well it was, but that would mean going way off course and I was determined to keep the boat going in the right direction. I have not come all this way to give up at the first hurdle.

What made it even harder going was knowing the future forecast – I was not likely to have favourable winds until Tuesday!! Tuesday, it's Saturday today!! Anyway, crack on with it I did and decided to keep with the 2hrs on, 15mins off pattern. It was hard graft but would get the job done. I worked out that by breaking the day down into smaller goals made the whole thing much easier to cope with rather than thinking "I have to row like this till Tuesday."

You can see from my tracker that I had to take a much more westerly route than I wanted, it was just too much throw into the wind.

Message from Charlie:

Time 11am, the next 48hrs is going to be tough but good winds are to follow. Wind light SE going S then no wind overnight. Sunday light S going W (headwind) then N later tomorrow and Monday AM. Then starts to fill in and settle . Expect N going NE on tuesday and filling in, by wednesday we should see good trade winds.

KEEP AT IT, AND IF YOU FEEL DOWN, REMEMBER, YOU CHOSE TO DO THIS!! HA HA. YOU ARE ACTUALLY DOING A GREAT JOB!

As the day went on the wind direction remained but dropped in strength so I was able to start coming a bit more south again. Problem was, as soon as I stopped rowing the boat would be blown West again, I was still rowing through treacle so I could only have short breaks or risk going way off course.

I reckon I rowed about 19hrs of that 24hr period!! That's not dipping your oar in rowing either, that's hard core, get-your-back-into-it rowing. All this and I was making hardly any ground, I had a few moments during the hours of darkness I will admit. "What in earth am I doing here? How am I going to keep this up for 49 days? I will be out here all year if things don't improve." I have found something out about myself that I never knew! I am actually a morning person?!? Who would have thought it?

No matter what hours I have been doing during the night, my morning routine is now:

- Straight on the oars at 06.30 for a two hour shift
- Stop for 15mins to get washed and changed into whatever I need for the day
- Start the next two hour shift feeling sorted and ready for the day.

Sunrise is about 8am so I get to experience the whole thing on my first shift.

It's amazing watching the sky turn from twinkling white lights to a lighter blue, as the stars start to switch off you can see where the sun will come up as the sky around turns pink. There are always a couple of stars that wait till the very last minute before switching off. Then when you think you must have missed it, pop, up it pokes from the horizon. I can immediately feel my shoulders loosen, my head clear and the whole epic task does not seem so daunting.

I save a special treat for my afternoon break. My lovely friends Molly and Rosie have written me a letter for every one week I am at sea. Today is my one week anniversary, and it really was brilliant to open something from home. This one contains a song which I am recording for your entertainment!! Thank you so much girls you are amazing young ladies. Xxx

As the night set in I can see clouds forming all around me, and a few hundred miles to the north I can see flashes of lightning lighting the night sky. Thank god I am not there, I think!!

Oh yeah, nearly forgot – started listening to Gary Barlow audio book. It's really good.

Day 7 0900hrs stats:
Past 24hr Distance 45nm
Total Distance 356nm

Max Speed 3.8kts
Min Speed 0.54kts
Avg Speed 1.88kts

13th January 2019

Sun and rain

Another amazing sunrise, another moment of "we can do this" and another day of putting in the hard graft. I have made a real push to try and get more South today, if you look at my track you will see me going South West, you can also see every so often a spell of going North West. This is because the wind is pushing me this way so whenever I stop rowing that's the direction the boat goes. When I stop I am not resting, there is always something to do in these 15mins. Clean the solar panels, make water, charge GPS or other electronics and remember to eat and drink enough.

About 10am it starts to rain, only a light rain but it's actually quite refreshing, there is blue sky all around apart from a patch of black cloud above me. You know what that means.. rainbows!! A beautiful full rainbow just for me.

During the day the wind shifts again it's now blowing from the North West which is even worse. This means that when I stop rowing I will literally be blown backwards. It's not a strong wind at all, but enough to take me off course and keep the treacle factor going.

Message from Charlie:

11.00hrs Remember the headwinds are the sign of change, so embrace them with love and they will turn into fair winds to push you along. Have a good day x

I decided I would keep my 2hr on 15mins of pattern until about 5pm when I would drop my anchor. Not conventional anchor of course as it's 4km to the bottom (I try not to think about that!!)

it's was a beautiful day so I had a vision of a bit of down time on deck taking in the sun whilst being held by my para anchor from drifting backwards.

The day was so nice that if it were not for the relentless rowing I could have been on a beautiful relaxing Holiday with flat calm seas.

The time comes and I unpack everything, this is a performance in itself as it consists of the parachute anchor in a bag, a bag of 70m of line to hold it and a bag of 100m of rope to retrieve it. I connect it all up as per my training and deploy the anchor. What is supposed to happen is that the parachute fills with the current under the water and as it is connected to the front of the boat then holds it in the tide against the wind. What actually happens is that I watch it sink straight down and as its bright yellow I can still see it at 20metres down! I start to have a bit of a very mild panic that a whale might get caught in it so haul it all back in. Now it's all wet of course it twice as heavy. By now I have taken 20mins and drifted about half a mile backwards. So I decided that the lines must be tangled preventing the chute from filling. I untie each point, untangle it and re attach it. Satisfied with my work I give it another go this time making sure the chute is inflated before paying out too much line. It fills and I let it out where I watch it sink straight down again!! Those of you that know me know that I don't have a lot of patience when things don't go right for me. So without really giving it a chance to let the wind take effect I haul the whole thing back in muttering something that I hope I didn't record on my go pro. Result.... no rest, an hour going backwards, over a mile lost and a pile of wet rope I now have to dry out before packing away.

On the plus side, I did get another visit from a turtle. Apparently nobody else (ocean rowers) have ever experienced this! Maybe it's the orange bottom of the boat? I feel very privileged.

I continue with my shift pattern into the night each time I stop losing more ground. I can't tell you how demoralising it is to work your socks off and end up further back than the same time yesterday. I have pulled out all the stops, worked beyond my own expectations and given it my absolute all plus more on top. Whatever the outcome of this journey I am very proud of myself.

Another day of hard graft tomorrow as the winds are predicted to be head on!! Flipping 'eck! I need to find another gear!!!

Day 8 0900hrs stats:

Past 24hr Distance 16nm

Total Distance 372nm

Max Speed 2.16kts

Min speed 0.54kts

Avg Speed 0.67kts

14th January 2019

Going overboard

Up and on the oars at 06.30 again as usual; feeling cold and demoralised. All that hard work and I'm now further back than yesterday lunchtime.

No point feeling sorry for myself, get on with it. Hunched up and head down I begin the familiar movement's legs, arms, arms legs driving the oars through the water with each push of the legs. It's not even a head wind yet, that beauty is for later!!

I look up at my wind vein which is all I ever seem to look at. It tells me everything I need to know about the weather! I have a similar weather prediction device at work in the rear yard – we call it the windy tree!

This morning I decided to play some music through my speaker via an iPod lent to me. I don't know what's on it so I put it on shuffle and hope for the best. It really cheers me up, one minute-Christmas music then heavy metal then zen whale music!!

Then something amazing happens, this morning's sunrise seems to be like a solar panel for my motivation. Once the sun is fully in the sky I feel invincible, combined with a cheesy 80's power rock ballad on high volume I am on top of the world. Nothing can stop me!!! I am enjoying every minute of this row today no matter what direction the wind takes. I have a few aches and pains by now, but nothing that a good stretch won't sort out. My hands are intact and generally all together I am in pretty good shape.

As usual I set myself small goals through the day with small treats. Today's treat is to go for a swim and clean the bottom of the boat!!! Oh no, I have been dreading this part!

At 3pm armed with goggles a go pro and a scraper I get myself ready to take the plunge. I have a good scout round the boat checking for any unwanted visitors, the coast looks clear so in I go. It's blooming freezing. Head under and have another look round. There is nothing but blue as far as you can see, so I crack on scrubbing the bottom. I want to get this over and done with as soon as possible. Every time my safety line touches my leg I shout "what the hell was that?!" And put my head back under for another look. I kept talking to myself and laughing at how stupid I must sound. Soon as humanly possible I was back on the boat getting dried and ready for some more rowing.

After a couple of hours rowing guess what I see? Yes a shark!!! It only looked about 5ft long but big enough to take your leg off. Everything else I have seen out here I gasp with excitement, the sight of a shark made me stop and gulp! I hope I never have to get back in that water.

Throughout the day the wind has gradually tracked round all the points of the compass, starting south then west (my head wind) then north by sunset. Hopefully overnight it will come round to the north east where I should be able to start making up some ground.

At 9pm I was writing this blog inside my cabin when I heard what sounded like heavy breathing coming from outside. As I went out I could see the moonlight shimmering off the backs of two dolphin as they surfaced to breathe. WOW!! It's an absolutely magical moment. There is no noise from wind or waves just the sound of dolphin which have a reassuringly human quality to the noise they make, like when you come up for breath after diving in the sea on holiday. I could see one of them swim under the boat silhouetted by the moonlight. Amazing moment.

Maybe it's a sign of good things to come over the following weeks.

Day 9 0900hrs stats:

Past 24hr Distance 21nm

Total Distance 393nm

Max Speed 2.16kts

Min speed 0.54kts

Avg Speed 0.88kts

15th January 2019

It's all a bit 'Meh'

Today has been a bit of a 'meh' day! By that I mean a bit middle of the road.

It was good to have the wind behind me at last, but still hard going to even get the boat above 2kts. It was all a bit overcast so the batteries don't charge as well, meaning less time for tunes on the speaker. I know the better winds are coming but it's another day trudging through the treacle factor to get there.

The very good news is that this time when I stop for a break I actually drift in the right direction! So was able to give myself half hour and 45min breaks in between shifts this time which is how I caught up on all my blogs.

I have had some great feedback about my blogs, I have been told it's like reading a book that the ending has not been written yet. I am glad I have taken the time out to do them as well. I bet if I had not written these and you asked "how was it?" I would not remember half this stuff, so it's great to have a record. Perhaps Angelina Jolie might play me in my film! Lol!!

Message from Tina:

Well you have brought tears followed by smiles reading your blogs. It has been emotional on every level. But I have loved reading it like a novel that leaves you waiting for the next chapter. Stay safe my nutty chicken. I am with you every step of the way. I will come up with a ditty for you. (I can not print the ditty as it was too rude!! Did make me laugh though!!)

Saw another turtle today floating by, this one didn't stop for a chat though. That must be 8 I have seen now. Am I exactly following some kind of turtle route to Barbados? It reminds me of the film Finding Nemo!

Rowing today has its own challenges to past days. With little wind it's been really flat water most of the time, which means I can use a really good technique, getting lots of purchase in the water and giving a good amount of propulsion with both oars.

Today as the waves are now getting up I am constantly missing a stroke, or a wave blocks the oar so I smack my shin with the handle. I guess this is another reason for feeling 'meh.' I was expecting a great day on the oars with the wind behind me. Instead I got just as hard a day with only a small increase in speed.

Oh well, overnight the wind should really kick in then the great catch up begins! I think I am about 180miles behind the world record pace at the moment, with a few weeks to go this is very achievable to catch up on. Bring it on!!!

My memory foam seat cushion lost its memory. It has been a godsend but is now flat as a pancake! I have managed to fashion a seat out of an inflatable fender and it's really comfortable! It's actually the most comfy place to sit on the boat now!! Off to get some rest now ready for the Aurora tomorrow!!! I am loving this adventure.

Day 10 0900hrs stats:

Past 24hr Distance 28nm

Total Distance 421nm

Max Speed 1.62kts

Min speed 0.54kts

Avg Speed 1.17kts

16th January 2019

Yeeee-Haaaaa!

I am actually moving again! What a great feeling to be on the move. I have got some work to do to make up the world record pace but it seems that I am up for the challenge!

I have had 3 or 4 small birds follow me all the way from the start. No idea what they are but it's nice to have them along for the ride. They look sort of like swifts? No more other wildlife today just lots of big waves.

Now this is more like it, although the last few days slowed me down I don't regret them at all. I would never had the moments with the turtle or dolphin without that lull in the weather. It also showed me that I can really achieve things that at the start seem too tough to handle.

There are some quite big waves out here, I would guess 20ft but it's difficult to judge. Everything looks big from a 21ft boat. I have taken some video to post when I get back. See what you reckon.

Now what is fun is surfing down the waves, I line myself up with one, put in a few power drives to get me to the top, then – yeeee haaaa! – see how fast I can get the boat down the other side. When the ocean sends you waves you just have to ride them!! Absolutely brilliant fun!

I have been getting word from Aurora HQ that there has been quite some support on social media especially a 'Facebook wave?' Thank you so much to everyone who is supporting me, please keep it going it really is helping.

In fact I was thinking this is a bit like the Truman show, only I know I am in it! My world extends to 3 miles around me like a big circle, and it's usually just me in it. But I know so many people are watching me and encouraging me along. The thought that you can all see my track is quite a comforting feeling and also means I have more reason not to slack as you will know!!

I look forward to catching up with all your messages when I get to Barbados. In the meantime I hope you enjoy reading my blogs and look forward to sending you the next one.

The chase is on!!

Day 11 0900hrs stats:

Past 24hr Distance 52nm

Total Distance 473nm

Max Speed 3.25kts

Min speed 0.54kts

Avg Speed 2.17kts

17th January 2019

Getting back up to speed

Getting some good speeds back up today, it's a real knack to timing the oars with the waves but when I get it right I can really see the speed going up.

A couple of the waves have caught me side on soaking me, which resulted in me shouting at the sky then laughing at myself!

I don't feel like time is dragging too much. What I have done already seems to have flown by, still not felt lonely or scared. I just know I have a job I need to get on with so that's what I do each day.

Life on-board is pretty simple and I am getting to appreciate it, no social media, no demands (apart from the ones I put on myself.) It just really boils down to making sure I eat and drink enough, get as many hours as possible on the oars to keep the speed going, making sure I do take some breaks, and keeping up with maintenance on board.

My biggest worry are my batteries. When it's nice and sunny they are easy as they charge up no problems and I can run everything I need. Tomorrow looks like it will be cloudy, so I just hope enough sun gets through to charge my batteries.

If I had to switch everything off it would not be a problem I could still manage, but it's nice to know I can charge electronics when I need to. So whatever higher being you believe in, if you can ask them to send me some sun I would be very grateful.

I have been doing some sums and as long as I don't get another patch of bad winds I reckon I am still in the running for the world record. Keep on tracking me, I reckon if enough people will me along it's got to make a difference!

As the night draws in the sky is still pretty bright as we are heading towards a full moon, it's incredible how much light it gives off!

Day 12 0900hrs stats:

Past 24hr Distance 67nm

Total Distance 540nm

Max Speed 4.35kts

Min speed 1.6kts

Avg Speed 2.79kts

18th January 2019

A miserable start

Today's tale of woe has a happy ending so don't worry as you start to read. But before I start, does anyone know how long boiled eggs keep? I just found six that I made up for the start of the journey and never ate!! Think I might give them a miss!!

This morning I started not with the usual Aurora (as you know, Aurora is Latin for Dawn) but with a great dark miserable morning, you could not actually tell when the sun was up, everything just became a lighter shade of grey!

Ready I got nevertheless into my full wet gear. Not only is this seriously effecting my tan for the arrival photos in Barbados, but it's also uncomfortable to row in.

Both my batteries are at minimum and the day of thick cloud does not bode well for having enough charge for tonight. Already feeling sorry for myself I bail out the bilge by hand as the batteries are too low to use the pump, the second I have finished a massive wave virtually fills it right up again, I am beginning to think nature itself has a vendetta against me. I start to row, the sea is very confused meaning there are waves from all angles so every time I put my oar near the water the handle gets smacked into my chest shin or stomach. Not only is this very painful but it has the effect of slowing the boat down which is obviously the opposite effect to what I am trying to achieve. Eventually after a couple of hours of being battered and bruised I decided to check my mileage, I have been really putting some hard work so hoped that news of a 70mile 24hr might cheer me up! Nope... I have only done 65miles. This just tips me over the edge, I decided that the world record was now out of my reach, being out here was pointless and I am just letting everyone down. I sat back in the rowing seat put my head in my hands and tried to force some tears out. They weren't coming so I looked up for inspiration, just then a big wave approached that I recon I could catch. I must have looks like one of those kids who are crying for attention then stop and grin when the see a sweetie!! I grabbed the oars and rowed to the top grabbing the wave perfectly. When you catch a wave just right it smacks the back of the boat like you would a horse to set it off running. As I flew down the other side with a smile on my face I realised I still loved the ocean and I am actually making some reasonable mileage so what's the problem, after all I stayed positive in the days I was going backwards!!

After texting Jaime I realised I had stopped setting small targets and what just thinking of this as a whole. So I got to work deciding on my new shift pattern 2hrs on 30mins off until I had reached 12hrs rowing. All seemed to be good with the world on the ocean again and the sun even came out to give me a bit more charge.

Morale of this story, if you have a massive challenge, break it down into smaller more manageable ones.

I saw a shark today, was literally about 2ft but I still don't want to be dipping my toe in at any point while it's around!

The wind is due to pick up overnight so hopefully will keep the mileage up. I tend to position the boat for the fastest ride during the day, but the most comfortable ride during the night so the speed does usually drop off overnight.

Still looks like more cloud tomorrow which is my biggest problem right now so if you can all carry on wishing those cloud away would be brilliant. But for now I will be finishing the day with a beautiful sunset and feeling positive.

Day 13 0900hrs stats:

Past 24hr Distance 69nm

Total Distance 609nm

Max Speed 6.01kts

Min speed 1.08kts

Avg Speed 2.88kts

19th January 2019

Another grey start

Today started in the same way as yesterday- dark, grey, cold and wet. As I sat on my rowing position in the dark I am not even sure if the sun is up yet as everything is covered in black cloud. I am wearing shorts and a waterproof top when all of a sudden the heavens open and I am totally drenched!

I just sit there not bothering to move as if I go in the cabin I will just make everything inside wet and I have done a pretty good job of keeping inside dry, tidy and cosy.

I just keep hauling the boat through the water, I don't know if I am in some kind of current against me as I just don't feel like I am getting the speeds I should be. With a following wind I should be able to get the boat above 2kts which I seem to be having trouble doing. I sit out the rain and eventually dry out but due to the constant cloud cover I never really get warm. I am already looking forward to my long break where I can get in my sleeping bag. Going back to my previous comment, I am not actually a morning person at all, I am a sunny and warm morning person! Hopefully as I get further south it should start to warm up a bit. Although be careful what you wish for, I have been in this cabin when it's boiling hot, it can get really hot!!

Message from Pammy:

I have just looked up at the moon and thought you could see it too. I am sending my love via the man in the moon.

I must stop adding up the miles and worrying about them. There is a long way to go yet, but I can't stop thinking I am out of the running if I don't keep up a certain pace and speed. The goals I set for myself today were to keep the boat above 2.5kts, because I have not kept that going all day I am really annoyed with myself. I need different goals for tomorrow as if the weather conditions don't allow me to row at that speed then there is no point having that as my goal. I think I will stick to my 12hr on the oars goal, at least I know this is achievable.

Well its two weeks at sea today so that means its letter opening day. I had a beautiful poem from Molly and Rosie which was absolutely wonderful and just the boost I needed to keep going. I will ask if they mind me publishing it on my next blog for you to read. You will see why I had a boost of energy after reading it.

I am surprised at how good a shape I am in physically. My hands are a bit dry and a couple of callous but no cuts blisters or anything that needs treatment, just a bit of hand cream every day. My shoulders and back are understandably stiff, but certainly not painful and I have had no need to take any painkillers so far. The majority of my fitness training was either on the water or on the rowing machine so I think I must have got the muscles used to what I am putting them through now. I even took my rowing machine on holiday to France with me, now there is commitment!

The day itself continued to be pretty grey with not quite as much wind as I would have liked, but all in all I am feeling fit and strong I just need a bit of sun on the situation to give me and my ships batteries a boost!!

I think it is or nearly is a full moon tonight but can't see it under the cloud.

Day 14 0900hrs stats:

Past 24hr Distance 68nm

Total Distance 677nm

Max Speed 6.01kts

Min speed 1.08kts

Avg Speed 2.83kts

20th January 2019

Pirates?

The whole day was cold wet dark and miserable! I have been rained on every day for about 4 days now, it's really not good for morale! It's not good for the batteries either, I need to make some water! I have managed to make enough to drink but have had to eat some of the wet ration food as I don't have enough water to put into my dehydrated meals. Don't worry I am sure I will have more than my fair share of sun once I get a bit further south, in fact I will probably be begging for cloud by then! Never pleased!

I have been getting some reasonable mileage in, but to be in with a chance of catching the world record pace I really need to be getting higher numbers, it's so frustrating putting all my efforts in and not getting the results I want. I suppose I should just concentrate on getting back safely as the weather is the deciding factor on this one and there is nothing I can do about that. I am just very proud of myself for keeping going every day and pulling it out the bag. I did want to be at home on several occasions today whilst cold and being rained on, but giving up is not an option for me after coming this far.

About 6pm I saw a yacht on the horizon, it was definitely getting closer. I could not see them on AIS or contact them via vhf radio? I tried for about half an hour to get done response but nothing? In the end I changed course just to make sure they passed well clear of me. I am sure they had no idea I was there so thought is safer to get out of the way. I also wondered if they were up to no good in the middle of the Atlantic with no AIS, even more reason! Here be pirates!!!

Day 15 0900hrs stats:

Past 24hr Distance 58nm

Total Distance 735nm

Max Speed 3.25kts

Min speed 0.54kts

Avg Speed 2.42kts

21st January 2019

Rowlocks and airlocks

I think it's Monday morning? I wonder what everyone at home is doing on this – you guessed it – wet, cold and cloudy day?

I have still been putting sun cream on my face as I know the cheeky blighter has a way of getting through the clouds and reflecting off the water. I am going to get back with very brown hands and face, and that's it!!

The day did not continue too well either. Firstly the water maker has some sort of airlock, so I only managed to get about 300ml out of it before I had to stop to let the batteries recharge. I just need to run it a bit with the valve open to bleed the air out. Hopefully I can do that tomorrow.

Message from Michelle:

You are doing amazing, we are so proud of you. We constantly follow you and are first to do every moment and last thing at night. Keep going fab lady xx M & M

Later on a massive wave caught me from the side. I let go of the oar to grab the rail, when the oar got stuck the wrong way, straight up and trapped by the current. With all my might I managed to free it, but in the process it has bent the plate that the row lock is attached to. It still works, but I can feel the oar is not entering the water properly now. I tried hammering it back into place, but it's just not shifting. In the end I had visions of smashing my hand instead of the hammer on the plate, missing and chucking the hammer in the ocean by mistake, or smashing a hole somewhere I don't want a hole. So I decided that I would just have to put up with it for the rest of the way. Oh just to add insult, I have rowed nearly 1000 miles with no blister…. I now have a blister from all the hammering! Doh!!

The sun made an appearance here and there during the afternoon and into the evening so I did manage to dry out a bit.

My mileage is totting up, which is great, but again I always expect just a bit more from myself. I will keep plodding on regardless.

All of your messages of support are getting through and they really do keep me going, I can't thank you all enough.

Day 16 0900hrs stats:

Past 24hr Distance 60nm

Total Distance 795nm

Max Speed 7.13kts

Min speed 1.62kts

Avg Speed 2.5kts

22nd January 2019

Flying fish!!!

No that's not me going nuts! My row before sunrise this morning was accompanied by flying fish. First I saw one small one, then another then a couple of big ones! I hoped none of them landed in the boat as some were getting quite some height on! They were not particularly graceful either, it was more like someone was chucking them from underneath the surface of the water rather than actually flying. But it was certainly a good distraction from what was to be another grey morning.

I am guessing flying fish only come out during the early hours as I didn't see any more for the rest of the day. Well, that is until about 11am when I turned to get my water bottle from the side pocket. One very small and unlucky flying fish had obviously not accounted for there being a boat in the way and was now stuck like some hideous hunting trophy on the bulk head! Yuk! I said a little prayer and sent him on his way back to the sea where he belonged.

Message from Jo Bird:

Hello Chicken. Me and Sophie are in ipswich tonight because Soph has her uni interview tomorrow. She says with an inspirational auntie like you she is gonna smash it.... if you can she can xxxx

Once the sun was up it was still quite dark, but I still did my morning ritual of standing up after my first rowing shift and looking out over the front of the boat. It gives me a chance to have a good stretch and just generally take in the amazing view which is our ocean. Each day is the same ocean but with a slightly different twist. This morning the sea looks dark with large waves breaking in the distance, other mornings it has been glassy flat with a reflection of the sky clearly visible. Just amazing! And just to add to the amazement of the view I see two dolphin riding through the waves ahead. They didn't come any closer, just passing through I guess.

Message from Sue: Sending more positive energy and love! We are in Tarifa, Spain in a motorhome on the Atlantic. So windy here and thought of you out there. Keep going Dawny xxxx Sue B

I got rained on a lot today until about 2pm when the clouds eventually cleared. At least I am getting good use out of my gear I suppose. Before setting off I had visions of embracing a rain storm by getting the shower gel out! Lol! It is so blooming cold I just keep rowing in the rain until it passes and can try and dry off a bit. Still I got another amazing rainbow.

Today's wind conditions were perfect. I got some great distance covered during the day and got to ride some brilliant waves. I absolutely love it when you are right on top of a wave and can see for miles, all of a sudden- whoosh- 6kts I clocked high speed today! Brilliant.

You may have noticed by my track that I am trying to get as far south as possible whilst still making forward progress to Barbados. This is because the further south you are the more likely you are to catch the trade winds. It's a decision anyone crossing the Atlantic should think about- the shortest straight route is obviously going to be quicker if there are no weather systems to deal with. The longer route (which I am taking) is less likely to have bad weather therefore should be quicker. However, as I have already found and looks like I am going to find again, the weather is something that will play its own game. All the apps and prediction software and the weather will still do what it wants.

As the evening draws in I am really pleased with the progress I have made, it's been my favourite rowing day as I actually felt like I was gliding the boat through the water rather than hauling it. I really started to feel at one with the ocean too, predicting where the next dip and trough were going to hit and at times riding a path almost like I was being shown the way.

However, all good things must come to an end! The wind is due to drop right off again overnight and the forecast does not look good for the coming week! I really need to start working out how I am going to pull it out the bag again to get through another bad spell of weather!

I decide to get some rest while the wind still has some forward momentum on the boat so I can get up early hours to start back on the oars for the heavy work.

Day 17 0900hrs stats:

Past 24hr Distance 58nm

Total Distance 853nm

Max Speed 4.9kts

Min speed 2.16kts

Avg Speed 2.42kts

23rd January 2019

More adverse winds!

And so, another stint of bad weather begins. Today through till Friday I should sort of have the wind behind me although overnight tonight I will have some south in it, if this pushes me too far north I will either have to put extra night hours in or deploy my para anchor. However, as it's such a light wind its back to hauling the boat rather than gliding it. Despite hours and hours of rowing during the day with little beaks I barely manage 1.5kts which is less than walking speed. It's absolutely soul destroying especially after the fantastic progress yesterday.

Message from Brenda:

Hi Gorgeous, just wanted to let you know you are doing so well. Both me and Kev are so proud of you. Keep it up darling, you have nailed this.

I was not on the oars from 9-11am as I had to get some repairs done. There is an electrical box from which the sealant had come loose so sea water was getting in, not a good combination!! So I spent two hours drying it out, spraying it all with contact spray then doing a job of trying to re-seal it. It's not pretty but I will eat my hat if any water gets in that. Another go on the water maker which is also still not playing ball- it runs for a few mins ok, then I have to open the valve and run it open (gets the air out but you don't get any water) for a few mins before repeating the process. It's a real battery drainer but I manage to get 2litres in the end. On the batteries- it's partly cloudy today so will have plenty of charge for tonight.

Anyway, back to the weather! After a couple of days hard graft, I have then potentially got an 18kts head wind for at least 12hrs. There is absolutely no chance of rowing against this, even the biggest and bravest rowers would not be attempting that. It will mean I have to go on para anchor which means no rowing and going backwards at about 0.3kts.

All of this is pretty tough to take in when I am really busting my gut to get through just today alone. I am really struggling to work out how I am going to work my way through this patch. I know I will as that's what I do but it's a very low point to think you have pulled out every ounce in the last batch now I have got to find some more.

Well I know what I am going to do first- get that speaker on at full blast with a bit of foo fighters! It might not help long term but right now I feel a whole lot better, I just hope I have all the Albums on iPod somewhere!

I have a chat with my weather guru Angus back at Rannoch HQ to confirm a bit of a schedule of weather times. It's not good news at all but I find it helps if I am fully armed with all the information so I can form a plan in my head of how to tackle this. One day at a time is the ultimate answer, so I plough on through today putting in lots of hard work with the intention of resting overnight ready to tackle another slow day tomorrow.

I must have sounded pretty negative to Angus by text as he told me 'You're doing so well you should not be so negative' and he is absolutely right. It's just that I have put so much work into planning and preparing for these weeks at sea it's pretty heart breaking to see part of the dream being taken away because of something out of my control.

Message from Angus:

It's cold as F**k here and brexit is killing me, I would love to be on a boat right now. Stop being negative, your expedition is going well, and you are doing a decent time.

However, this campaign has so many goals it's not just about getting the record. I want to inspire others and this next few days will give me the opportunity to do that, show the world that even a normal person like me can overcome the seemingly impossible.

I can't help feeling down about this latest setback, but I do promise I will get to the other side of it. I am going to need to get that speaker back on full charge for tomorrow.

Day 18 0900hrs stats:
Past 24hr Distance 57nm
Total Distance 910nm
Max Speed 4.9kts
Min speed 1.26kts
Avg Speed 2.38kts

24th January 2019

Happy and S.A.D.

When I look back on this adventure this is one of the days I want to remember. I absolutely loved today, it was just brilliant. I still worked really hard rowing for a total of 12hrs, driving myself through every inch of the ocean, but I decided to ignore the mileage for today.

The wind conditions simply do not allow me to clock up big miles and over the next couple of days I may even go backwards. But, there is nothing I can do about it so I may as well crack on and enjoy the experience. Don't get me wrong, I am still totally gutted to see my goal of holding the world record slowly reducing in possibility, but I have put this part further down the pecking order otherwise I will miss out on enjoying this incredible achievement.

What made today so good? Well for starters I had sun and lots of it!! I reckon I have that SAD disorder you know, even when a cloud goes past my mood drops slightly!

Having sun means firstly I am able to take my blooming wet gear off and dry it out. I can also dry my trainers out – sorry I know I am a lady but these trainers are bogging!! (Bogging is my word for stink like a rotten bin bag!!!) It's not fun putting your feet into cold wet bogging trainers every morning!

It also means fully charged batteries, which in turn means fully charged speakers and iPods. As soon as my speaker was good to go I had some of my favourite tunes on the go – the best ones included anything by Foo Fighters or P!nk.

I have made a go pro video of me singing along, looking forward to sending it to P!nk herself to see if she likes it!! Having music playing is a real boost and when the nearest person is probably over a thousand miles away I can turn it up as loud as I want!!

The water was teaming with big bright colourful fish all following my boat along. I had company all day, you can see them quite far down too. I got some good footage of them under the boat. I had not really thought too much about what's underneath the surface up until now. The water is such a dark blue that it's easy to forget there is life under there. I also saw an electric blue long thin fish but don't think I got him on film. I would tell you what they all are but Google does not work out here!

Message from Dad:

Hi Sweetheart we are thinking of you and praying that the conditions improve. We are watching your track all the time. Good Night God Bless love Mum and Dad.

As the sun starts to set, I turn the music down and choose some chill out tunes. If it were not for the fact I am using my own human power to get this boat along I would have thought I was on holiday. A really lovely end to the day.

Now I have made it sound like I have been sitting on the aft deck drinking G n' T all day!!! This is very much not the case when it comes to the rowing, I have hauled myself every inch of today's mileage putting in tons of grit and determination. I am feeling pretty proud of myself for yet again finding the sort of power and will needed to do this today, knowing I would have little distance to show for it.

I have not ever thought about giving up, nor will I in the future. I am sure, however, that I will have more days when things seem overwhelming and tough. I may need some encouragement as I am only human, but one way or another I will find a solution and get to Barbados! Ohhhh, a nice cold beer right now would be amazing! Sorry got distracted thinking about Barbados.

Anyway, tomorrow is due to be another tough day, I might even have to deploy the dreaded para anchor! I will keep you posted how that goes.

I am about to go into the night shift – I really love rowing under the stars! – but will be getting a few hours kip in before the morning to make sure I am ready to tackle whatever comes my way.

Look up at the stars tonight as I will be too. Reach for the stars, you never know, you might just catch one. Signing off from a very contented boat, all be it a bit tired and aching.

Day 19 0900hrs stats:

Past 24hr Distance 29nm

Total Distance 939nm

Max Speed 2.16kts

Min speed 0kts

Avg Speed 1.21kts

Photographs

Rosie

Gloriana

Great River Race

Kay 'TAV'

At work on Alert IV   *Launching in GC*

Week 1 letter   *Week 1 at sea*

 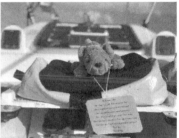

Cleaning the bottom   *'BERT'*

Marvin the Marlin   *Terry the Turtle*

Getting shade   *Sunrise (Aurora)*

Keepsakes   *Navigation*

'Suns out Guns Out'

*Meeting with SV LOLA and a few days
later with SV Orinoco*

Battling waves   *Barbados bound*

A beer at sunset   *Nearly there*

Stepping ashore

A warm welcome   *MCS t-shirt*

Martin and Su   *Amazing gift*

25th January 2019

Frustration

Well this morning started well, got a nice sunrise and didn't get hit by any flying fish (although I did find another dead one in the bilge), all was going well in the world of Aurora.

Gradually as the day went on, rowing became tougher and tougher as the wind started to shift from east to south, then to South West. The wind strength also gradually increased until eventually, by 1pm, I was rowing with all my might and only making 0.5kts. Time to get out the dreaded para anchor.

Now it transpires I have an incredible fear of my para anchor!! Some people have normal fears like spiders, oh no not me!! I have a fear of catching a whale or shark in my anchor. I wonder if I am the only person on earth with this fear. Can I name it?

Honestly, all the massive waves and gnarly ocean I have rowed in without fear and loving every moment over the past few weeks, and this is what stumps me!

To explain, if you are rowing into a headwind and can't make ground then you deploy a parachute (para anchor) into the water which is attached to the front of the boat. This holds you in the wind so should only be pushed back at a rate of 0.5kts rather than 1.5 or whatever the wind strength is. You can't row with this in the water, it's simply a way of slowing your backwards progression. Then you just sit and wait for the wind to change.

It's pretty frustrating not rowing or progressing forward but for me having that blooming thing in the water is also really scary!

I desperately try to think of ways I can rig it up with some sort of quick release mechanism. I send Angus from Rannoch (my shore team) loads of messages asking if I can rig it here, do this, do that?

He must think I am suffering with scurvy or something as I am sure he never encountered these questions. Anyway, funnily enough the reason the boats are set up as they are is because this is the best and safest way to do it. So eventually I conceded and set the para anchor out as it should be.

During the night I try to get some sleep as I won't be doing any rowing, the wind is getting up to 20kts and will be directly head on.

There was definitely no sleeping happening tonight! The noises in the boat were loud, no different to other windy nights, but this time I was very conscious of having 40m of rope hanging out the front of the boat with a parachute attached to it.

Every bang, every swoosh of a wave, every creak of the boat I assumed was the dreaded anchor getting snagged on something. It was relentless all night. I wish I had filmed myself now as it would be like that scene from Blair Witch Project! But at the time I was too scared to think about it.

All in all, another frustrating day ending in being scared of my anchor. But…. I still find a way to get through it and gradually conclude another day.

Day 20 0900hrs stats:

Past 24hr Distance 28nm

Total Distance 967nm

Max Speed 2.16kts

Min speed 0kts

Avg Speed 1.17kts

26th January 2019

Overcoming my fears

This morning started with such dark clouds that it was hard to tell if the sun was up or not!! It absolutely poured it down from about 5am till 9am. I suppose that's one of the good things about being on para anchor is that not being able to row, I did not have to go out in the rain. The headwinds were now up to 20kts with absolutely zero chance of being able to row against it so I just had to sit and wait for a window of light winds to try and catch some miles up.

Now it was daylight, all be it dark, I was feeling a little less anxious about the para anchor, well actually I just tried to forget it was there. I don't really know where this had come from as I am normally pretty realistic about things and use evidence based information to make judgments and opinions on things. I have never felt scared or alone during this experience as I know I have planned everything so well and have drilled my emergency procedures so many times, this is something I was not expecting. Anyway I have resigned myself to the fact the anchor is staying out till at least the afternoon and I was not going to be rowing.

I listened to a bit of an audio book I have started, I did some cleaning, clearing, checking and packing away, and I did something that changed the mood of the day for the better (I was not feeling bad or low, just keen to crack on and row) I washed my hair!!!! Last time I washed it was the day I got in and cleaned the bottom of the boat, I think that was well over a week ago. I am living with it so I smell amazing to myself, but I wondered if anyone was with me they might think my head was starting to resemble the odour of a sheep! Oh my goddess it felt great to rub shampoo in my hair and get a good clean up and put some clean clothes on. Wonderful.

Now I was really ready to face the day. At 1pm I hauled in the para anchor and began to try and row against the headwind! With all my might I drove the right oar through the water in an attempt to point the boat in the right direction, as soon as I reached the desired heading of 230degrees I joined in with the other oar. As the wind caught the nose of the boat it just kept going round. Now I had to drive with all my might on left oar to get the boat straight again. Basically, I was doing a speed of 0.2kts and just spinning in semi circles! This was achieving nothing so I had no choice but to put the para anchor back out.

After a couple of hours I tried again with the same result, so I tried to get my head down for a bit so I could row into the night if needed.

I have now been a sea for 3 weeks! I can't believe how quickly it has gone! Three weeks means my weekly letter from Molly and Rosie. This one did not disappoint, in fact it was almost like they had predicted what I would be going through and chose some encouraging words to match. My favourite line is "life can be tough, but so are you!" Wow that is exactly what I needed to hear and do you know what, I am beginning to think it's true. Life does not always bring us what we want, but we need to stay strong so we can face those things. Just amazing thank you again girls.

I had a chat with Charlie this afternoon, Charlie is a seasoned ocean rower, founder of Rannoch adventure and helping me with my weather routing and shore support. He told me that you can't beat the weather so you may as well work with it, if you can't row then get some rest. I was beginning to worry that people would think I was giving up because I was not rowing, this reassured me that there is nothing I can do in a headwind other than prepare for when it changes.

My window for rowing is overnight when the winds are still on the nose but drop right off, so I am writing this on my 10pm 15min break. I will report tomorrow if anything exciting happens after this blog, but basically I am aiming to get 10-15miles in overnight while the winds are light. They are due to pick up again tomorrow so will assess then if I will be able to carry or rowing maybe with an adjustment of course or deploy anchor again. Fingers crossed Monday night I should be back to following winds.

Finally, before I sign off for the night, I want to introduce you to Bert, he is doing a very good job of looking after me. He is not usually allowed on deck but as it was calm I let him out for 20mins. My lovely Daddy lent him to me but wants him to come home safe with me. (Bert is a toy dog)

Day 21 0900hrs stats:

Past 24hr Distance 10nm

Total Distance 977nm

Max Speed 2.16kts

Min speed 0.54kts

Avg Speed 0.42kts

27th January 2019

Looks like I am in for a sunny day today. lots of water made, batteries charged, and iPods to the ready. Only problem is still this wind!

The wind is now coming from the south making it firstly slow progress, and secondly pushing me northwards, which is the opposite to what I have been trying to achieve over the past two weeks. I was quite impressed with my almost perfect circle on the tracker I created whilst on para anchor though!

I start off making reasonable progress against the wind, but as the wind strength increased throughout the day it became more difficult to row against it. Going northwards is not ideal but at least I am making forward progress. On para anchor I would not be making any headway at all. So the day really consisted of nice sun, good tunes but slow going. Monday night should be when the winds start to turn so hopefully if I keep pushing on I will be in a good position to start picking up speed again.

Message from Jaime:

You are doing amazing considering the wind you have got! Love you baby xxxxxx

Message from Zoe:

Hello lovey Dawn. I have been looking after your social media and have some stats for you. In the last 28 days the posts have reached 73.3 thousand people! 75.3 thousand people have engaged with the posts and 947 new people have liked the page. The impact you are having is immense xxxx

I have been getting word that there is so much support out there, especially changes people are making to help reduce single use plastics. I can't thank you enough, it really makes all this worthwhile I have been hearing of community beach cleans, changes to shopping habits and so much great work happening. I am so honoured that what I am doing really is making a difference.

Today I saw a green plastic bottle float past, unfortunately too far to grab it. I thought to myself that I am in a spot on earth where very few humans have ever been and yet we have managed to pollute it. The changes we are all making all add to the bigger picture to make the planet a better place for us all. Thank you again for getting behind me.

Day 22 0900hrs stats:

Past 24hr Distance 27nm

Total Distance 1004nm

Max Speed 2.16kts

Min speed 0.54kts

Avg Speed 1.13kts

28th January 2019

Wet Through

Today should be my last day in the slow lane, it has started very dark and ominous!! The sky is thick with black cloud and just as I am getting ready to sit down to row, there is a flash of lightning shortly followed by the biggest clap of thunder you have ever heard crashing through the sky.

With no buildings or obstructions in its way the thunder seems to roll from far away on my left, across the front of me then off to the right and into the distance. I watch the sky following where the sound is coming from but don't see any more lightning.

The whole rest of the day had a very dark feel to it with massive outbreaks of rain every hour, I was literally soaked through and through. The cabin has started to get damp inside now, there is not a lot I can do about it really, but am doing my best to keep the electrics and charging cables dry and at least keep a dry patch for me to sleep in.

Rowing today is again hard work as the wind begins to shift, hopefully by this evening the trade winds will have started to fill in and I will be on my way again. I have done some calculations and I think that the world record time is still achievable but would require some fantastic winds for the rest of the crossing which is possible but not likely.

Anyway, I have decided that you should never give up on a dream so I will continue to push myself and put every effort in, but I still won't let it consume me and ruin my experience. A wise man once told me "better to reach for the stars and miss, than reach for the gutter and find it." I want to get to the finish line knowing that I tried my best and fully deserve the title of 'Ocean Rower'

(or 'Dengie Warrior' as apparently named on Facebook!! I quite like that!!)

Into the evening and it's still dark and gloomy, but with a smile and a 'wave' (see what I did there) I row out the night pushing every last mile I can, looking forward to meeting up with the new weather system.

Day 23 0900hrs stats:
Past 24hr Distance 23nm
Total Distance 1027nm
Max Speed 2.71kts
Min speed 1.08kts
Avg speed 0.96kts

29th January 2019

Shades of Grey

It's been days since I saw a sunrise! The past few days have just been different shades of grey (isn't that a book?!) depending on what time of day it is, today is no exception. But nothing can dampen my spirits today as the wind is changing in my favour.

Overnight and this morning were still hard going but with the expectation of some faster days coming up I got my head down and kept at it. During the morning I passed a quite large piece of fishing net about 10m off my port side. It was very lucky I did not get tangled in that. Fishing net round my rudder would prevent the boat from moving properly and if I could not release it could be an expedition finisher.

About two hours later I passed a rather large yellow buoy, I am not sure if they are connected but I was lucky not to hit either- thousands of square miles of ocean and I nearly run into them both!!

By the afternoon an ominous whistle starts to sound around the boat as bits of rope, aerials and safety lines start to move with the quickening of the wind speed. Within an hour I had what I had been waiting for, and some!!

With 33kts of wind now blowing it was one hell of a ride. The waves I am sure reached 20-25ft at times, it's a real art to getting this right or I could capsize the boat. I have to manoeuvre the boat to make sure that each wave catches the boat from behind, picking it up like a toy car then shooting it off over the other side.

I am pretty sure I hit 9kts at one point which is pretty impressive for a rowing boat. However, if you see Charlie from Rannoch, it was at least 20kts as he pledged £10 for every knot over 5.5 to my charity the Marine Conservation Society.

This was a very exciting, adrenalin fuelled afternoon, I was in my element!! There was often a rogue wave that would hit from the side and send the boat sideways setting the whole deck completely awash.

It's been hard work at times whilst rowing on a flat Ocean just to reach 1.5kts. Now I was doing an average of 3.6kts and it's still hard work but in a totally different way. I have to have my wits about me at all times staying as safe as possible whilst heaving the oar through the water to change the course of the boat ready for the next wave.

I have very good seamanship skills and never take anything for granted when it comes to being at sea, so everything on deck and in the cabin was tied down, secure and in its correct place meaning I lost nothing overboard. Well I thought everything was secure!!

I have 5 lockers in the deck of the boat where I store my food. Each locker has a round watertight screw on lid – well they are watertight if you do them up properly.

I noticed that my ginger nut biscuits seemed to be tapping at the see-through lid, as if to try and get out? Erm, that's not right? That locker is only half full so I should not be able to see anything at the lid height. I realised that the locker was full of water just as a gummy sweet snake swam past the ginger nuts. As I took the lid off I could see that it was full to the brim and everything inside, including 5llb of gummy snake sweets, was swimming round in it. Now comes the task of bailing it out. Keep in mind I now have 20ft waves, the deck quite often being awash and the boat not always being level.

I quickly emptied out the food content onto the deck and began to bail as fast as I could before it filled up with water again. I don't know how, but apart from a couple of small splashes I managed to empty the locker of water and re pack the undamaged food pretty quickly and without anything going overboard!

Needless to say my daily checks now include ensuring the hatches are tight. It's so easy to loosen them with your foot as you go past.

This amazing wind and thrill ride lasted well into the night and as much as I want it to stay its pretty exhausting.

It does not matter what the conditions are like, out here it is going to be a tough day, if it's flat calm extra strength is needed to drive the boat through the water, or strong winds bring other challenges to deal with the conditions. This is an incredible challenge and one I feel grateful to be experiencing, I have worked so hard to get here and will take in every last part good and bad.

Until tomorrow land lubbers!

Day 24 0900hrs stats:
Past 24hr Distance 40nm
Total Distance 1067nm
Max Speed 3.25kts
Min speed 0kts
Avg speed 1.67kts

30th January 2019

Emails gone wrong!!

I have an email account set up on my old iPhone which shrinks the size of the file so it can be sent via my satellite phone. I have been using this to send these blogs. A few days ago it gave up the ghost- I suspect it got damp. Today I managed to work out how to email from my iPad, so I have been trying to catch up and somehow managed to merge two days into one by mistake! So the 29th of January is actually the 30th with a bit of 29th thrown in. I am now back on track, so the next blog is in the correct date.

Day 25 0900hrs stats:
Past 24hr Distance 74nm
Total Distance 1141nm
Max Speed 19.1kts
Min speed 0.54kts
Avg speed 3.08kts

31st January 2019

An anti climax!

Well after yesterday's excitement today was a bit on an anticlimax! I am now use to life on the superhighway, I am certainly not back in the slow lane (I am very happy about that) but I defiantly have to work for my miles today. It's cloudy but not raining at least, so I put on some nice clean clothes and my waterproof trousers over the top. This is firstly in the hope my waterproof trousers will dry out during the day and also the seat is soaking wet and I am not putting my clean lady pants straight onto that!

I start to row and start to consider the condition I am in. I am pleasantly surprised when I go from top to toe. Head- mentally I am coping pretty well with this, I have had a couple of melt down days but got over them pretty quick when I gave myself a talking to. I think I would be more worried if I didn't have a couple of bad day, you would have to be a robot to spend time at sea like this and not let it effect you. Shoulders/arms- Not too bad at all, back and shoulder muscles coming along nicely, my right elbow has a bit of an ache but nothing serious. Back- I thought I would have real trouble with this, but I have been really strict to keep good posture all the time which has really helped and, touch wood, other than a little stiff it's all good. Hands- very good, I have been moisturising every day and apart from a few callous (very ladylike) they are in great shape. Bottom- the seat I made myself a couple of weeks ago is still going strong and has worked a treat. I have heard horror stories of blisters and unmentionable things on ocean rowers bottoms but again by keeping good care of myself has paid off. Legs- my knees are starting to feel it, it's like doing hundreds of squats every day as the power comes from pushing with the legs. It's not bad enough to need to take pain killers but I will certainly keep a close eye on it. So all in all I am basically a fully functioning rowing machine. Having the will power to get on the oars hour after hour day after day is probably the biggest challenge, but I am doing it. Not only am I doing it but I am exceeding my own expectations of how I would cope.

As the day goes on I spot some massive fish jumping out of the sea. I have no idea what they are but remind me of when you see salmon jumping. These fish must be 3ft long, they just launched about 4ft in the air and belly flopped back in the ocean! Of course as soon as I grabbed my camera they stopped, but honestly they were quite something to watch. If one of them landed on me I would know about it.

As the day closes I am just taking a break to write this blog before doing my last 2 hour shift I have rowed 10hrs so far today so that will make up my 12 that I do as a minimum every day.

Before I go I just want to say a massive thank you to a few people. As most of you know, I have run this campaign virtually single handedly from social media to accounting to event organising, I have had lots of wonderful friends help with a few bits and pieces but essentially it's just been me. So I was a bit worried that you would all forget about me when I set to sea and could not stay in touch. Well I have been proven very wrong. My wonderful friend Jeremy Smith has been receiving these blogs from me and passing them on to you as well as doing an amazing job of looking after my website. My amazing sister in law Zoë Stow who has looked after all my social media, I can't thank you enough. And my fantastic Dad Barry Smith who by the sounds of it has a Star Trek style Aurora HQ operations room set up at home with my mum where emails have been flying back and fourth and all kinds of amazing contacts are being made- I am fully expecting the Queen to meet me in Barbados for the grand arrival.

Right this is eating into my rowing time, Look to the stars,

Day 26 0900hrs stats:
Past 24hr Distance 59nm
Total Distance 1200nm
Max Speed 8.27kts
Min speed 1.08kts
Avg speed 2.46kts

1st February 2019

From best to worst

Today went from one of the best days to one of the worst. It started with a little glimpse of the sun so I started up the water maker for the first time in a couple of days. This still is not running right, you should just turn it on and get water (about 4litres an hour) but I have to keep bleeding air out of mine. So I run it with the valve open for just as long as running it closed and end up with half the amount of water, in fact today as the clouds came back in again I got less than a litre. Hopefully tomorrow I will have some sun (I have said that virtually every day.)

What was going to make this the best day is that with a bit of welly I was making over 3kts average, if I can keep this up I will be back in the running. As you can probably guess, I did not keep up 3kt average. At almost midday exactly I slowly began to lose speed. I put it down to the wind dropping slightly and carried on ploughing through regardless. As the afternoon went on I continued to get slower and slower whilst putting in more and more effort. This was not how I planned this day going, I was imagining sending out messages saying how well it was all going, not worrying about my speed.

Things gradually got worse as my seat suddenly stopped moving – two of the wheel bearings had gone. There was now black stuff all over the deck and shortly all over me. Luckily I had packed spare bearings so I set to work changing them and fitting them back on the seat. To someone who knows about this sort of thing it's probably a 10min job, but I had to work out how to get the old ones out, then by trial and error fit the new ones in. This took up about an hour and a half in the end, which was time I should have been rowing my ever slowing boat.

I wondered if more weed had grown on the bottom of the boat, it's far too choppy to get in and clean it so I rigged up a scourer on a rope which loops under the boat, and holding one end either side of the rope and pulling back and forth cleans the bottom. The only problem being that this does not work at the rear of the boat as the rudder is in the way. I then spent another half an hour trying to get as far down as I could whilst staying on the boat to scrape round the rudder end but despite my efforts I did not really make any difference.

I was eager to get back on the oars as I had missed a lot of time doing DIY, but decided to set up the auto helm ready for tonight as I would be needing it. This was my next big issue!!

During the strong winds the other day the spare auto helms became dislodged and the one that was plugged in had been hit by the others. All the cables were loose in the bottom which of course by now has a small amount of water in it. The one that was in the mounting was also now wedged fast and took me a good half hour to get free. Once I eventually got the chance to test them it looks like only one out of the three now work, this is not good news at all.

By the time all this has happened it is now dark and I will have to continue my investigations of the rudder in the morning, I am not hanging over the side of the boat in the dark.

I am just setting down for a rest, writing this blog, when I also realise my back is now pretty sore from heaving on the oars in a bid to keep up the speed this afternoon.

I am so disappointed as I was determined that today was going to be the start of my bid to catch up to the pace, but now I am just looking forward to some daylight so I can get to work trying to solve some of these problems.   I hope to bring you a better blog tomorrow.

Day 27 0900hrs stats:

Past 24hr Distance 65nm

Total Distance 1265nm

Max Speed 4.35kts

Min speed 1.08kts Avg speed 2.70kts

2nd February 2019

A month at sea

One month at sea today!!! It honestly does not feel like it, it's pretty much flown past! There were days I wanted to last forever and days I could not wait to end, but I would not change a second of it as without the lows I would not have appreciated the highs and I don't think I have ever felt like I have earned something quite as much as this. I think I will be at the half way point in about 3 days, however I am hoping time wise it will be another 3 weeks ish (assuming no more bad weather) I am still keeping my eye on the world record as I have worked so hard for it it's difficult to loose hope of a dream. But, I am desperately trying not to keep checking and re calculating as every small set back makes it hard to stay positive about the expedition as a whole.

The last couple of days I have had an electric blue coloured fish with yellow fins follow me along. He comes right up alongside the boat under my oar. You an see him coming as his colour makes him stand out in the much darker colour ocean. Occasionally he will swim off and dive through a wave but he keeps coming back. I have got some footage but the colours don't do it justice.

Talking of fish- I now realise the ones I saw the other day belly flopping were not flying fish at all. I have seen lots over the last couple of days and they do actually fly. It's amazing to watch, they are also a beautiful blue colour and just glide for ages before gracefully diving back in. I saw a group of about seven of them all flying along together earlier, so are they a flock or a shoal?

Sadly I also saw some kind of take away packet go past, I am annoyed I didn't see it in time, that would have been a good name and shame!

It's been pretty cloudy and overcast today, but enough sun managed to get through to charge the batteries enough to give my speakers a charge and also burn my face!! As I am I long sleeve top and waterproof bottoms I forgot to put sun cream on my face and now look a bit panda eyed.

I have continued to push hard on the oars again and feel I might have made a reasonable progress today, it's still not the mileage I am really aiming for, but, you can't fight the weather. I will continue to try my very best and be proud of what I achieve.

The seat wheels seem to be holding up which is great. I did some work on the auto helms by trying to clean out the sockets with contact spray, there is now power going to both the broken ones, but one will not set correctly and the other runs ok for about 30mins then turns itself off. Looks like I am stuck with just the one. Oh yeah, the water maker is still getting air locks but I got a good 2.5litres out of it this morning, so battery allowing, I will hopefully get more tomorrow.

I have been stretching plenty today between shifts so my back is also feeling much better, and am back to all systems go. Today being 4 weeks means I get to open my next letter from Molly and Rosie. This one has a song about rowing and some jokes. They really made me laugh and was a great little treat for my afternoon break, these letters have really given me a boost and something to look forward to every week.

There are always going to be things that don't quite go to plan, but all in all I am feeling happy, healthy, fit and strong. Nearly half way there and am ready for the push home.

Day 28 0900hrs stats:
Past 24hr Distance 55nm
Total Distance 1320nm
Max Speed 6.01kts
Min speed 0.54kts

Avg speed 2.29kts

3rd February 2019

A near miss

I just had a flying fish go past my face about a foot away!! If I had been at the catch rather than the end of the drive I would have been knees bent, slid forward, and the thing would have smacked me clean in the side of the head! It's also a good job it had some height or it would currently be decorating the side of the boat!

Wow, I have seen so much fish life today. My blue mate with the yellow fins has brought some friends along to see the strange lady rowing mid Atlantic. At one point there were about eight of them. The belly flop fish have been jumping all around the boat (every time I get my camera out they stop) and the flying fish have been travelling round all over the place in groups.

The last couple of days I have also seen big balls of sea weed floating past. Sadly I also saw a plastic lid off a large tub float past – I keep logging these in my blogs as when I get back I can do a report of what I have seen at each location across the ocean. It will be interesting to work out an idea of how much stuff is floating in our oceans and devastating to think what has already sunk below.

My water maker made about 5 litres today without (touch wood) too much trouble, so even if it's cloudy tomorrow I have a good couple of days' worth to keep me going. The sun even made a bit of an appearance today, not much but enough to go short sleeve. I can actually start to feel the temperature start to rise a bit the further south I go, although sometimes I do wonder if I actually took a wrong turn and am in the North Sea with all the cloud and rain there has been.

I really do feel comfortable and at ease out here on the ocean, I love the sounds the sights and how each day brings something new. The sea state at the moment is pretty moderate, so not the exciting surf waves that I love, but it does make for better living conditions. I have been much less likely to get drenched by a wave or try and move round the boat without getting washed off your feet. It does mean slower going than I would like but I am just taking each day as it comes and working the conditions as best I can.

I have been listening to an audio book today while rowing which really made the time go. It's a 15hr book which I finished a short while ago, so that's 15hrs rowing today. Still feeling fit, strong and healthy, so let's see what tomorrow brings. I am ready for you!!!

Day 29 0900hrs stats:

Past 24hr Distance 59nm

Total Distance 1379nm

Max Speed 8.27kts

Min speed 1.08kts

Avg speed 2.46kts

4th February 2019

All downhill from here?

Amazing day on the Ocean, I am absolutely in my element out here. The flying fish are coming past thick and fast now. It's not going to be long before I am hit by one I am sure. My blue friend has now also been joined by a big green fish. I wish I had brought some sort of I-spy book of birds and fish so I could identify some of the wildlife I am seeing.

The other thing I wish I had done was downloaded more audio books. For the first couple of weeks I hardly listened to any music or books, I am very happy with my own company so didn't really feel the need to, I just wanted to take in the sights and sounds around me.

On the very few occasions the sun has been fully out I have loved putting on some power tunes to motivate me to row that extra bit longer or up the power just a bit. Ibiza chill out tunes on sunny calm evenings are a nice way to finish a day, but mornings until midday are reserved for the sound of the ocean.

On days like today, not too sunny and not too many waves to challenge the brain, I have enjoyed a few audio books. Today was Dawn French – what a brilliant lady. But, that was the last one I have. The only other thing I have talking wise (I have lots of music) are some ghost story podcasts and real life crime. I am not sure listening to ghost stories on a small boat on my own in the open ocean is such a good idea!!!

I got in and gave the bottom a really good scrape off. There were lots of things growing on it, a lot of which I must have missed on my last bottom clean. I can't believe so much has grown in such a short time. I started to get a bit apprehensive about getting in again, when in the end I just said to myself "either get in and do a

proper job, or don't be surprised when the boat slows down."
This time I got right under the boat and got off every last thing
clinging on.

Well, I am still ticking off the miles and think I will be half way
maybe tonight? I will double check in a minute. So hopefully now I
am on the downhill stretch. I am loving this experience but am
starting to look forward to a long hot shower and a cold beer – in
either order!

Day 30 0900hrs stats:

Past 24hr Distance 60nm

Total Distance 1439nm

Max Speed 6.01kts

Min speed 0.54kts

Avg speed 2.50kts

5th February 2019

Mid Ocean pollution

Before I start, I forgot to mention yesterday that I saw a plastic bottle and a plastic egg box shape blue box. Today I saw a blue bottle screw top. I have logged the positions, I am just putting them in my blog to remind me what the items were.

This campaign is aimed at highlighting the problem of plastic pollution in our oceans. I am simply astounded that slap bang in the middle of the Atlantic Ocean there is clear evidence of the sheer scale of the problem. Not one corner of our planet is safe from the damage us humans are doing to it.

Please help by making even just one change such as, don't buy bottled water, buy one reusable bottle and just refill it every day. Find out if you have a local milkman, you will be supporting a local business and reducing your plastic footprint. Swap to soap bars in the bathroom, there are so many to choose from now so you will smell lovely and get rid of plastic bottles from your bathroom. There are lots of other ways to help, but these are just a few for starters.

Message from Tom S:

Its great you scrubbed the boat, that took a lot of bottle. You have shown exceptional talent and courage from day one. Love ya to bits.

On to today's adventure. I have passed half way! To celebrate I ate half a packet of Jaffa cakes!! I should have brought a miniature wine bottle or something, but Jaffa cakes were a perfect celebration meal!!

stalled a fish pond overnight, the ocean is
fish doing out of it and in my boat? In front of
ll where I keep my buckets, it generally fills
, ume a wave washes over the boat but just
_u> bailing out.

So as usual this morning it was full of water, but when I inspected it there was a fish swimming round in it. Good news is he seemed fine, so I scooped him up in my bucket and replaced him back into the sea. I will still be amazed if I get across the ocean without being hit by one.

The morning started cloudy, and as usual I got rained on, however it's now warm enough to not really let it bother me. By mid-morning the cloud cleared and I had a beautiful sunny day to row to. As the saying goes "suns out, guns out" so out came the guns (that's arm muscles if anyone thinks it's something rude) and I am now officially beginning work on my tan.

My trainers have given me a very strange foot tan, so I have now cut out the tongue and part of the sides so I still have the heel and toe I need to give grip in the foot plates, but more air can circulate. They are a bit like a cross between trainers and flip flops... I shall call them 'Flipners.'

Still making good progress, although I really am putting everything into it. I really don't know how I keep doing it with a smile on my face? Whilst training for this I did do quite a few 2 and 3 day sessions, but I was always pleased to get home for a shower and a stretch out at the end of it. Out here it's day after day with no let up, but I am enjoying it. I will of course re visit this at the end!

Well, moving into the night shift now so I'm getting my head torch and jacket ready, and of course look forward to my long break which I save for night time in my cosy cabin.

Day 31 0900hrs stats:

Past 24hr Distance 64nm

Total Distance 1503nm

Max Speed 7.13kts

Min speed 1.08kts

Avg speed 2.67kts

6th February 2019

A beer at sunset!!

Quite an eventful day really, which has led to me writing this blog whilst having a beer! Yes, that's right, a beer. To find out how the day has ended like this keep reading.

Firstly, my daily plastic spot which was a blue unidentifiable piece in some floating seaweed and what looked like the lid from a large paint pot. I am usually too late spotting anything to get a chance to grab it, I am determined to get hold of something in a bid to find out where it has come from and how many miles it's travelled.

 I have seen another sunrise at last!!! This is the first day in ages I have not been rained on and the sun has been out all day. Blooming marvellous! Once the speaker was charged the tunes were on and the singing was loud. The wind is still pretty moderate but with a bit of welly I am knocking off more miles. The current forecast is for less wind at the weekend (boo!) but then it picks right up from Monday (hurray!) However, all the wind is going the right way so I am definitely not complaining, there is just more chance of higher mileage the more windy it is.

There were no fish in my pond this morning, but I did have a close encounter with a fish this morning. A massive wave took me by surprise from my left hand side. It literally swamped me and the whole boat. As the boat levelled and the water cleared I was left with a fish in my lap. This is absolutely a true story. I have made it sound like a massive tuna landed on me. Actually the fish was about 2cm long, but it was still a fish.

Later in the afternoon, I spotted a sailing vessel coming up behind me, I double checked its course via AIS and was happy that it would pass at least 2 miles clear of me. Then I noticed it seemed to be changing course.

"True Blue this is LOLA on channel 16, over"

"LOLA this is True Blue receiving you, over"

"True Blue, we have just changed course to come over and see you. Are you a rowing boat?"

"Yes, I am a solo female ocean rower on my way to Barbados"

"Wow, this is amazing, can we come over and take a photo? Can we bring you some fresh fruit?"

"I am not sure how we would get it over, but fresh fruit would be very welcome, see you shortly".

A few minutes later I was joined by the wonderful crew of LOLA which was a very beautiful Yacht. I am guessing about 55ft, but I am a very small 21ft so I may have misjudged that. The crew were a lady who I was talking to on the radio and two guys who I am guessing were father and son (again I was not too close, so could have got that wrong.)

Now, my crossing is solo and unsupported. This means I cannot have any kind of organised support. For example, if I run out of food and arrange for a boat to drop me some off that would make my record attempt void – however if by chance encounter you are offered something you are permitted to accept.

So the plan was arranged via the radio that Lola would put some fruit into a dry bag with a rope and small buoy attached, this would be thrown in up wind and I would retrieve it from the water.

Attempt one did not come close enough, attempt two I did not grab in time, but attempt three was a direct hit – the bag came right alongside. I was so very grateful, and the thought of fresh fruit was just brilliant.

We wished each other a safe passage and may even catch up in Barbados if they stop there, it was very strange to interact with people – such a brilliant encounter.

As they reset their sails and went back on their original course I opened the bag. Oh My God!!!! Oranges (perfect) apples (lovely) cheese (just wow) chocolate (not just any chocolate, Dairy Milk!!) and two beers!!!!!

Beer!! It's like someone actually heard me and delivered my shopping list!!

So that's how I come to be drinking a beer whilst writing this blog. I am having one now as a slightly late half way celebration and I think I will have the other one at sunset on my last night on board.

So a very happy Aurora is signing off for another night.

Day 32 0900hrs stats:

Past 24hr Distance 62nm

Total Distance 1565nm

Max Speed 6.57kts

Min speed 1.08kts

Avg speed 2.58kts

7th February 2019

Melting chocolate challenge

Not much to report today, no close encounters of the fishy kind and no visitors bringing beer!

It's been a bit overcast today with a few spots of rain, but still enough sun to keep my spirits up.

The wind seems to have picked up slightly today, and if it were not for my two spells of bad weather, this would be perfect wind speeds to get me comfortably within world record time. Unfortunately, despite pushing the limits to regain some ground I am still about 2 days behind the pace, so I really need some stronger more challenging conditions to close the gap.

There are very light winds predicted over the weekend which is not good news at all, but from Monday it should pick up again. With just over two weeks to go it's a long shot that I can catch up, but the fat lady has not sung yet so I will continue to put every effort in until the last minute.

I had an orange with breakfast and lunch today, I cannot tell you how good they were. To have eaten nothing fresh for a month then bite into a juicy orange was just heaven. I have also eaten the whole 600g dairy milk bar. It was starting to melt so I had to act fast. Don't worry, I got it all in time.

Then as an after dinner treat I opened the cheese. Wow! I have no idea what sort of cheese it is but my goodness it's amazing. I reckon I ate 200g of cheese so let's hope I don't have weird dreams later. The only thing that would have made the cheese better would be a glass of port... Let's see what the next passing yacht has on board!

I am starting to feel the effects a little now. My fingers are a bit stiff, my hands are holding up well, but despite lots of moisturiser they are very dry. And my bottom – it's definitely not getting picked for the next tennis player poster. I am still fit and healthy, but 12 hours per day rowing is starting to catch up with me.

Well that's all my news for today, stay tuned for the next instalment on board True Blue.

Thank you everyone for your continued support, it really does make a difference knowing that everyone is routing for me.

Message from Dad:

Wishing you a good night. Sleep Tight. Lots of love Mum and Dad xxxxx

Day 33 0900hrs stats:

Past 24hr Distance 64nm

Total Distance 1629nm

Max Speed 5.45kts

Min speed 1.62kts

Avg speed 2.67kts

8th February 2019

Rehearsing for Barbados

Another day at sea, I am glad I have these blogs to look back on as I think the whole thing will blur into one once I am home. It will be good to remember the ups and downs and some of the amazing sights. I still really want to see a whale, I am not sure how I will feel if I do, scared? Emotional? Excited? Perhaps all rolled into one.

Message from mum:

Good morning from Aurora HQ. Another brilliant Blog. Saw Jaime last night he is doing ok and looking forward to seeing you. Off to see Gary tonight as he has a gig, Love Mum and Dad

I am beginning to run out of things to listen to, I actually resorted to a podcast of myself talking about the challenge which was recorded back in the summer. That was strange sitting on the ocean listening to myself talk about what it was going to be like.

I have also put my iPhone music on shuffle. This has been great because it throws up some random songs not part of any album. When I was in my band I would download odd songs to rehearse, so this brought back loads of great memories of gigs I have done. I miss singing in a band, I might have to do something about that when I get back.

I am still putting every effort into getting as many miles in per day as possible, but I can feel it starting to take its toll. My knees and elbows are aching, as are my fingers. The seat has just had another layer added as this is now becoming uncomfortable, and general tiredness. I am actually pretty impressed that it has taken this long to start really feeling it.

I am not in any pain and am still in good spirits, I just need to get up and stretch every hour now as opposed to two or three. But with hopefully just over two weeks left, I know I don't have too much longer left to keep going. Anyway, standing up for a few minutes has given me the chance to practice my celebration photo poses when I arrive in Barbados.

Tomorrow marks five weeks at sea which has gone so fast. It's been amazing so far but I am secretly glad I don't have another 5 weeks ahead (I hope.) I am starting to look forward to coming home and luxuries like a flushing toilet! Although, it is amazing how fast you get used to a non-digital existence without Google or social media, it's actually quite nice to have a very simple existence.

My blue fish friends have not been seen for a couple of days, so apart from a lot of rowing I don't have any maritime stories to bring you. Let's see what tomorrow brings.

Day 34 0900hrs stats:

Past 24hr Distance 65nm

Total Distance 1694nm

Max Speed 6.01kts

Min speed 1.08kts

Avg speed 2.71kts

9th February 20

Five weeks in

5 weeks today since I left Gran Canaria, I r
This has been such an amazing adventure with my pa
is the Ocean. Now I am getting closer to land I am starting to wonder some things....

1. Will I be able to walk when I get off the boat? It struck me today that although I stand up every day to look over the bow and have a good stretch, I have not actually walked anywhere for five whole weeks. My calf muscles seem to have become smaller and when I flex them they don't seem as powerful. I will be doing a few leg days in the gym when I get back.
2. Will real life seem overwhelming? I have really enjoyed my own company with the odd message here and there to friends and family, apart from that I have had no calls or emails or pressure from anything that normal life brings. My days consist of making sure I have made enough water, make sure I have enough food, look after myself, look after the boat and row like a crazy rowing woman day and night hour after hour! Apart from the odd bit of music or audio books that is my simple life right now and I love it. I hope I can manage all the piled up work that will be waiting for me when I get back.
3. What next? I will answer that one when I have had time to recover and reflect!

It's been a beautiful sunny day, so that always puts me on a high. But the wind has gradually eased off over the course of the day. There is now not much more than a light breeze so overnight will be tough going with little mileage to show for it. I have learnt that there is nothing I can do about the weather so I will just get as many miles as I can and enjoy the calmer conditions whilst I have is quite nice to be able to sit on deck typing this, watching ars appearing as it gets darker, without constantly being mbarded with waves and washouts. The lighter wind days also make spotting wildlife easier, which leads me to my next part of today's story.

Message from Shelley:

Hey Chicken, glad all is ok. Loving your blogs they are amazing, you are amazing. Keep going and looking forward to seeing you when you get back. xx

About 4pm the sun was now round almost behind me, so if there is anything in the water, the sun will reflect off it. Suddenly I can see something large and blue following directly behind the boat about a foot away. At first, I wondered if it was a baby whale? Then I thought it may be a large dolphin as it moved in the same kind of way, but it was not breathing on the surface as all the others I have seen have done. Then as it came along side I could see its massive long beak…. a Marlin!! Wow!! I grabbed my go pro camera and stuck it in the water, I managed to get a glimpse of it on camera and also got a reasonable still from it. I will try and attach it to this blog but the quality gets compressed via satellite. It quickly shot off after that and did not see it again for the rest of the day.

My favourite part of Saturday is now my weekly letter from Molly and Rosie. I yet again was not disappointed. This week was telling me to never give up and dream big. Very, very wise words, ones of which I will defiantly stick to. I also got a little mascot who now sits with my other good luck charms. I want to send pictures of everything but I just don't have the data to be able to. I will send what I can then share the rest when I get back. Thank you again for reading, I hope you enjoy getting them as much as I enjoy writing them. Dream big, and never give up.

Day 35 0900hrs stats:

Past 24hr Distance 60nm

Total Distance 1754nm

Max Speed 4.35kts

Min speed 1.62kts

Avg speed 2.50kts

10th February 2019

Yet more plastic!

Today unfortunately brings more plastic. There was some kind of white thing floating about 100m away from me. I am not sure what it was but it was quite big, maybe a discarded fender? Also another plastic water bottle floating on the surface followed by some seaweed with what looked like thin rope and bits of plastic all wrapped in it.

Unfortunately I can't collect any of it (I think my boat would be full by now if I could) as I am facing backwards and I don't ever see these things until they are past me. As you have seen from a few weeks ago, when I had to drop para anchor and ended up going backwards, rowing into a headwind is not feasible, which is what I would have to do to turn round and go back for things.

The winds have continued to drop from yesterday and there is now hardly a breath of wind. This has made it very hard going today and is extremely frustrating. I am rowing as hard as my body will allow and the hours go into the night, but the mileage tally does not reflect the effort. I am praying to the wind gods that it will start to pick up again tomorrow. Other than the wind, it's been another great day on the Ocean; nice bit of sun with broken cloud so I don't totally frazzle and regular visits from sea birds all day.

As it's hopefully my last calm day, I decided to give the bottom one last clean. I am actually pretty ok with getting in now. As long as I have my goggles on and can see round me I am pretty comfortable in the water. I use to do a lot of scuba diving and it's the same with that, once you are under and can see what's going on there are no surprises to worry about. I should have taken a photo of myself though as I must look pretty odd.

Picture the scene, go pro on my head, goggles on, scraper in hand, and peg on my nose!!! For some reason, maybe I have bigger nostrils than everyone else, I cannot go underwater without water getting up it. I either have to hold my nose or put a nose clip on. I did not bring a nose clip, but I did bring standard clothes pegs, so that is what I have been doing when scraping the bottom.

It's amazing how many barnacles have grown since its last clean. With my new found confidence in the water I managed to get right under and scrape off every last one. So True Blue is now smooth bottomed again ready for some super-fast speeds during the week (fingers crossed!)

The sunset this evening was beautiful, there was still a fair bit of cloud dotted around the sky. As the sun set every single one shone bright red. This then reflected off the water, and for a few minutes it was like looking through a red filter. Truly amazing.

Well, before I sign off I just want to say thank you all again for your support. I have heard there are so many of you following my journey, I am very humbled thank you. May your dreams come true.

Day 36 0900hrs stats:

Past 24hr Distance 48nm

Total Distance 1802nm

Max Speed 4.35kts

Min speed 1.08kts

Avg speed 2.0kts

11th February 2019

The temperature is rising

The wind has started to pick back up again today, I hope it will continue to develop over the next few days. If it does it will mean a nice swift passage for the last third of the crossing.

I can feel that the temperature is rising too, in the evenings now it's quite a nice warm breeze coming through. I still have to put a jacket on of a night-time but then I do feel the cold.

There has been a real increase in the amount of seaweed, it goes past in great big long runs. At one point I realised I was sat in the middle of half a rugby pitch size patch, I slowed right down as I tried to drag the boat through it.

I really hoped that none of it ended up round the rudder as that would mean getting back in to clear it.

I check the bottom of the boat every few days using my GoPro camera on a stick, so a lot of my footage is of the bottom of the boat. I will have to check it all when I get back in case there was something lurking in the background that I missed!

Once through the field of seaweed I did the same with my camera and was pleased to see it was clear.

I am not really sure what time zone I am in now? My phone has not updated so is still on UK time, by my phone sunrise is now 9am and sunset is 9pm so don't think I am that far out, maybe a few hours. I have now eaten all the fruit, cheese and chocolate (the chocolate went the day after) I am really sad about that. Eating the oranges was such an amazing treat from the usual food. With the cheese I was giving myself a piece every two hours as a treat, so that did not last too long either.

The good news is I have a beer left, I am still saving this for my last sunset.

Everything is still good, although, I am keeping up my stretching as I am definitely feeling the effects now. I think I might sleep for England when I get back. There is not much more to report today, other than rowing a lot and staying positive. Keeping my fingers crossed for a trouble free remainder of the crossing.

Day 37 0900hrs stats:

Past 24hr Distance 45nm

Total Distance 1847nm

Max Speed 4.35kts

Min speed 1.08kts

Avg speed 1.88kts

12th February 2019

Chasing rainbows

I feel like I have spent this crossing trying to find the end of a rainbow! There always seems to be that elusive windy day that never quite comes.

This time last week I was in a 'good' bit of wind, enough to start racking the miles up but not enough to get the really big miles, then the news of light winds over the weekend with the promise of great winds from Monday (yesterday) so I dragged the boat through it to find that yesterday was not a lot better and today was ok but dropped right off again this afternoon.

I am absolutely not moaning, I could be going backwards or sat on para anchor again or in the UK freezing cold!! So this is great to be moving forward.

It's just trying to explain how each day comes and goes with expectation of the following day's weather, but you still don't really know what it will be like till the day comes.

There is a line from the film Good Morning Vietnam they ask for the weather and he replies "Got a window? Open it!!" That's pretty much what you have to do, take each day as it comes and deal with what you find.

Today there has not been a cloud in the sky and I have loved every minute. Rowing the minimum 12hrs is getting tougher, but no matter what, I will see it out till the end. I have not done all this to start cutting corners now.

During the lead up to my row I attended quite a few open days and events to meet people and spread the word about what I am doing. You would not believe that some people actually seemed to come up to me just to tell me their negative opinion on it all.

I get that some people won't think much of what I am doing, but those people should walk on and keep their opinions to themselves. I had one guy who wanted me to tell him exactly how many miles I would be rowing and how many I would be 'drifting' because in his opinion it was easy – you just get in the boat and eventually end up at the other side. I wish I could magic him here for a day on his own. He would not last five minutes!

I have earned every inch of this crossing and have worked so hard to get where I am, nobody can take that from me. I would have some choice words if I saw him again!

My day was brightened up even more by the amazing discovery of an 80's album on one of my iPods! Ha ha, just brilliant!! I rowed into the sunset this evening to the sounds of 'Tiffany' I think we're alone now! That was a very good find.

Well that's me signing off for another day, as always hoping for more wind tomorrow! But also as always I will play with whatever cards are dealt to me and give it my best effort.

Oh nearly forgot, today's plastic spot was a bottle top. Goodnight from 852nm short of Barbados!! Nearly there.

Day 38 0900hrs stats:

Past 24hr Distance 58nm

Total Distance 1905nm

Max Speed 4.35kts

Min speed 1.62kts

Avg speed 2.42kts

13th February 2019

Caught a corker

I have been getting up some decent mileage today and hope to keep this up over the next couple of weeks into Barbados.

The waves picked up a bit this afternoon, most of which were coming from behind the boat although there were some rogue ones coming in from the side. One particular one caught me a corker. I was not expecting it and it tipped the boat right on its side putting the deck completely awash. I dropped the oars and grabbed on to the side rails just in time, I was fully expecting it to go right over but luckily it sat back upright with me still in the boat.

I am connected to the boat at all times when out on deck by a safely line connected to my waist harness. I never take this harness off, not even when in the cabin. This way if I have to get on deck quickly I can just clip on straight away. My PLB (personal locator beacon) is also connected to my waist harness, so no matter where I am that is with me.

The boat is also designed to self-right if it did ever go over. Its airtight cabins either end will just pop the boat back up the right way. In fairness the earlier wave was probably not big enough to tip the boat right over, but at the time I was dangling sideways in the ocean I did automatically brace for it.

During the day it's still pretty warm so over the next few days of strong winds it's not much of an issue getting wet, it's actually quite refreshing. But in the evenings and hours of darkness, being wet with a wind blowing and no sun to warm you up means getting a bit chilly so I will be at least in my waterproof top over the next few evenings.

I am hoping to get some good surf waves over the next few days too, so will make sure my camera is set up ready. I already had a 6.5kt run down one this afternoon, so let's see if I can beat that.

Other than the usual rowing, today I have also been double checking the stowage of all my kit and making sure everything is in its right place and strapped down. I have come this far without losing anything overboard, so I hope to come back with everything I left with.

I also had to do some work on one of my gates (the bit the oar sits in) one of the spacer clips had come off and the bolt started to come loose. This is the most nerve wracking thing, hanging over the side of a rocking boat with a set of spanners that you don't want to loose and praying to whoever will listen that none of the bits fall off and into the ocean. It's almost like a generation game style challenge! I did of course manage to sort everything out without losing any parts and my spanners are safely back in the tool bag. I am all set for the next few days and looking forward to the final push into Barbados. A little way to go yet, but the finish is definitely getting closer and becoming more of a reality.

As I write this I have 784nm left to go, I can hardly believe it myself and I have done it, I have rowed 2040nm!!! That's pretty amazing.

Dream big

Day 39 0900hrs stats:

Past 24hr Distance 67nm

Total Distance 1972nm

Max Speed 6.57kts

Min speed 2.16kts

Avg speed 2.79kts

14th February 2019

Romantic meal for one

Happy Valentine's Day. I hope you have had a romantic day. I had my usual dried meal for one with a lovely glass of sports drink to go with it.

Food for the day is not quite as good since my fresh fruit and cheese have gone. But generally my main meals are dehydrated, so just add water. They are actually not too bad, my favourites are posh pork and beans or spicy pork noodles.

I then have snacks in between like protein bars, nuts, biltong, biscuits and chocolate bars. I also have energy drink powders and tablets to add to my water bottle every day to keep my energy up. There is obviously a requirement to keep my nutrition up, but treats like the biscuits and chocolate add some much needed energy and just simply something nice to eat and to look forward to.

The wind has picked up slightly, so hopefully this 24hrs should give some reasonable mileage. I did have high hopes that this week was going to provide amazing wind conditions to give me a few days of big miles so I can catch up a bit, but it does not look like this will be the case. I am taking this all in my stride now and just enjoying being out here, and knowing each mile is another step closer to my goal.

I keep putting the camera on for a few mins each hour, I will share it when I get back so you have an idea of the conditions. I keep missing the really good bits though. I caught a brilliant wave this afternoon, it broke just under my stern and for a split second I wondered if it was going to take me sideways, but it picked up the boat, I tucked the oars in and off we went.

I clocked 12kts going down that one!! If I catch it right there are normally a couple of smaller ones that follow it up to keep the run going. Yeee haaaa!!

I don't know if your skin gets softer being out here, but I am starting to pick up a few cuts and grazes. Mainly on the tops of my legs from the seat rubbing. I have plenty of first aid kit on board, so am keeping on top of it all to prevent any infections. Good job it's winter when I get back to the UK, I will look like a patchwork quilt in shorts and t-shirt!

News is in that my family have booked their flights in to meet me in Barbados. It's making it all seem real that it's getting towards the end. I am definitely ready to get back to dry land to see my friends and family and some creature comforts (flushing toilet) but I will miss being alone with the ocean it's an incredible place to be.

I always start these blogs thinking, nothing's happened, what am I going to write about? Then I end up writing loads. So I hope my wild ramblings have kept you entertained, as they have definitely helped me take stock of what each day has brought to the experience.

Day 40 0900hrs stats:

Past 24hr Distance 71nm

Total Distance 2043nm

Max Speed 6.01kts

Min speed 2.16kts

Avg speed 2.96kts

15th February 2019

Toilet talk

I am quite a Tom boy is some ways, but I can also be quite ladylike. For example, ask anyone who knows me and they will tell you I cannot stand toilet talk and farting, it's absolutely horrible. But, here is a toilet story too good to keep to myself.

I was doing my morning chores, making water, cleaning out the fish pond, changing over the auto pilot that sort of thing, when I was thinking about the world record. I do still have a chance, but with 168 miles to catch up in a week I have to face reality that it may not happen.

So I starting thinking how there must be another way to get one, after all isn't there a record for sitting in a bath of beans?!? So there must be something I am the first at or quickest at. I carried on pondering whilst getting ready to use the bathroom. (This translates as put a bit of water in the poo bucket, put it on deck and sit on it.)

So there I was sitting on my bucket when all of a sudden there was the answer right in front of me. Literally right in front of me!!! A massive wave came up the stern of the boat which was going to go one of two ways – either topple the boat on its side or I was going surfing. Whichever it was had the potential to get me in the s**t.

So I gripped on to the safety lines one either side and tried to put as much weight as I could on the bucket to hold it still and stop it from going over. And you guessed it, I went surfing.

The 15ft wave picked up the boat sweetly and sent it careering down the other side with me perched on the bucket clocking a speed of 11.5kts. Once at the bottom the boat levelled out and I was able to continue my duties without incident.

I just can't get the image of what it must have looked like out of my head! My eyes big as saucers as I realised what was about to happen then laughing my head off as I surfed a wave trying to grip a bucket in place with my buttock muscles!!

Now surely there must be a world record for toilet surfing???

After all that excitement, I then finished getting ready for a two hour rowing shift. There were a few more big waves today with a little more wind, I did manage to get some footage, but the really good ones were when I was not filming.

As the afternoon continued the wind again began to drop off meaning less speed and a calmer sea state. I quite often think I have seen things in the ocean when it's just the shape of a wave or the colour change from cloud cover. I was thinking this when I saw a fin shape just a foot from the back of the boat, then as it dipped down again I realised it was a fin! It was not a dolphin or shark but I am pretty sure it was another marlin as the fin was the same shape. It didn't hang round long but was a little creepy watching it's fin circle behind the boat for a minute.

My album of choice for the sunset shift tonight... Luther Vandross. Great stuff, you can't beat a bit of Luther, although probably should have had him on yesterday for my Valentines evening.

As I write this blog the wind has dropped right off so I expect I am in for a long night. It's just so frustrating I have already rowed for 12hrs since six o'clock this morning getting some good mileage in, now with light winds if I don't put more hours in that will all be wasted. I am forecast reasonable winds for the coming week, but as we all know you don't always get the weather predicted.

Please send me all your positive wind thoughts to get me to Barbados safely and in good time, where I am due to become the 7th woman ever in history to row solo and unsupported across the Atlantic Ocean. (And maybe the fastest person to surf whilst sitting on a bucket)

Day 41 0900hrs stats:

Past 24hr Distance 73nm

Total Distance 2116nm

Max Speed 12.01kts

Min speed 1.62kts

Avg speed 3.04kts

16th February 2019

Thank Crunchie it's Saturday!

The wind picked up slightly in the early hours of this morning, so I was able to get a couple hours rest before beginning the day which marks 6 weeks at sea.

Imagine everything you have done over the past month and a half and then imagine spending all that time alone on a 21ft boat rowing for a minimum of 12hrs per day (usually more) in blazing sunshine, pouring rain, no wind, 33kts of wind and whatever else the elements bring. Let me tell you this has not been an easy journey, now I know why hardly anyone has ever done it.

I am struggling today. I have a headache which I think has been caused by not drinking enough water and not wearing a hat yesterday. I have obviously upped my fluids and put on a hat today but too late for the headache.

I have also pulled some kind of muscle just under my rib cage so it's pretty painful to row. Despite all this I have no option other than to get on the oars and row. Every hour I am not rowing puts time at the other end and now the end is in sight I am really excited to get there. Up until this point time has flown by, now time seems to be going very slowly. I am starting to run on empty and need to find some reserves as I still have a week to ten days to go, I know I will find it but it's going to be a long tough slog.

What did brighten my day was finding a pack of Crunchie bars I forgot I had packed. That was an amazing find. I actually shouted "oh my god, Crunchies!!!" I don't know who to, but it was worth shouting about.

I was also really pleased to hear about my mum and Lucy taking part in a litter pick in my neighbouring town of Maldon. The event was organised under the row Aurora campaign and 16 people turned up which is amazing. Thank you to everyone who took part especially my Mum and Lucy from the happy hearts keep fit class. What better way to keep fit than go on a litter pick.

I also got to open my weekly letter from Molly and Rosie, this one was drawing of countries, so if I get lost I can use these. I only have one letter left to go. They really have helped me to mark each week and give me something to look forward to.

Well I am hoping to get some rest in tonight to get rid of this headache, so I am keeping my fingers crossed for an uneventful evening. Hopefully a bit of rest and minus a headache might make tomorrow a bit easier going.

Day 42 0900hrs stats:

Past 24hr Distance 67nm

Total Distance 2183nm

Max Speed 11.5kts

Min speed 2.16kts

Avg speed 2.79kts

17th February 2019

Getting back my Mojo

I am starting to get my mojo back again today. Everything is still tough going but the light at the end is getting brighter. Headache has eased slightly as has the rib pain, so hopefully will be back to normal tomorrow.

I had another visitor today, sailing vessel Orinoco. I could see them in the far distance then realised they had turned round and were making their way towards me.

"True Blue this is Orinoco Chanel 16"

"Orinoco this is True Blue receiving you"

"Do you have two persons on board?"

"Negative, I am a solo rowing vessel"

"What type of vessel?

"Rowing"

"you have no sails or engine?"

"That's correct, just me and my oars"

They went on to check I was ok and to see if I needed anything to which I asked if they had any fresh fruit. As the yacht got closer they explained that they would pass across the front of my boat and drop the bag in front of me to collect. Direct hit first time. I got another delivery of oranges apples and cheese.

This is absolutely amazing and what a great boost to enter the final week with. I was half tempted to ask for a beer, but the one I have left is definitely enough I will save myself for when I get ashore. Honestly, I don't know why people worry about being out here, it's like getting your supermarket home delivery on a weekly basis!! I can't thank the crew enough, it was exactly the boost I needed and helped to break the day up perfectly. I just need to try and not eat it all in one day. They told me they were also heading for Barbados, so maybe I can thank them again in port.

Looks like its back to a full moon tonight. It's amazing how bright it is without any other light pollution it lights up the entire night sky. The ocean all around me sparkles silver as the moonlight bounces off the waves.

I am hoping to get a few hours rest during the night again to try and rid the last of this headache, luckily the evening is quite cool so the cabin is quite a pleasant temperature. As you can imagine it gets pretty hot inside during the day with no air circulation and the hot sun beating on the outside of the boat.

Day 43 0900hrs stats:

Past 24hr Distance 67nm

Total Distance 2250nm

Max Speed 6.57kts

Min speed 2.16kts

Avg speed 2.79kts

18th February 2019

Migraine strikes

This will be a short blog as I am struggling to look at the screen.

My headache has turned into a full blown migraine. If you suffer with these too you will know the pain I am in right now. My right eye can barely open, bright light makes the pain worse and makes me nauseous, heat and moving also make me feel nauseous.

If I were home, I would be laying in a cold dark room sleeping it off, but this is not an option. I have managed to row with a wet towel over my head and dark glasses, I can manage about an hour and a half before needing to lay down again.

Message from Gary:

Hey big sis, can't believe you are nearly there!! Mum and Dad will finally calm down! Your blogs and you are awesome! Superstar luv u xxx

Laying down does not bring huge relief as it's pretty hot in the cabin during the day with no circulating air, and it's moving. At least now the sun has gone down it's a little more comfortable, but I am not feeling very good at all. I am keeping everything crossed it passes by the morning as this is not a very nice experience at all.

Sorry it's a short one and hoping to bring you better news tomorrow.

Day 44 0900hrs stats:

Past 24hr Distance 70nm

Total Distance 2320nm

Max Speed 6.01kts

Min speed 2.71kts

Avg speed 2.92kts

19th February 2019

Sticky situation

First thing this morning I thought I was going to be in a sticky situation. My migraine was as bad as ever, the rowing conditions were tough struggling to get up any decent speed and the wind had shifted direction so keeping a good course was not easy. I had to start rowing before sunrise to get a couple of hours in before the sun came out to make it a bit more comfortable, I had to go to my happy place in my head on more than one occasion during the morning.

As the sun rose I realised it was going to be a pretty cloudy day, this is not good news for my batteries, but at least I would not have blazing sun on my fragile head.

Throughout the day my migraine has now downgraded back to a headache, and although I have not managed the mileage I would have liked, I am pretty impressed with myself being able to even get on the seat and go through the motions, let alone make any progress. It's amazing what you can achieve when the option to give up is taken away.

I have had odd hours though the day when the wind suddenly picks up for a short while making rowing a lot more comfortable. I obviously still have to row, but it's more like assisting the boat through the water rather than forcing it. More of those please for the final sprint to the finish. I have less than 400 miles to go now, I can almost see the palm trees. With a bit of luck today will be my last Tuesday at sea, this time next week- dry land, hot shower, cold beer, comfy bed!!

On this day two years ago I was in Hong Kong after just completing an Ocean rowing expedition along the coast of China. I was not rowing, I was part of the safety boat team so spent the two weeks at the helm of the Ribs (rigid hulled inflatable boat). I had been going out to China during the year leading up to the final expedition as part of the training team teaching Chinese students. During this time I taught navigation, first aid, seamanship and also skippered the 5 person rowing boats during training sessions. I absolutely loved the experience with Rannoch adventure, having the opportunity to teach in the ocean rowing world definitely started my love for the sport. Two years on, here I am writing a blog from my own ocean rowing boat in the Atlantic!!

Well I am feeling much more comfortable this evening, so have high hopes for a great day tomorrow.

I don't have long to go so I intend to enjoy every last minute.

Day 45 0900hrs stats:

Past 24hr Distance 59nm

Total Distance 2379nm

Max Speed 5.45kts

Min speed 2.16kts

Avg speed 2.46kts

20th February 2019

Top form

I am feeling on top form again today. Migraine gone, suns out and ready to tackle the last 350miles. I still kept my big hat and shades on as I do not want a return of that thank you very much. Lots of water and I can get a bit more food down now I am not feeling nauseous. I really did have a good bit of power going on today too, the wind was a bit up and down so I made a real push when it dropped to keep the momentum going.

Today is the day I had planned to be ashore and celebrating. I don't know why I picked 46 days it just seemed like a nice number to aim for. Despite closing the gap from what at one point was over 350miles to just 145miles today, I just had too much bad weather in the first couple of weeks to close it completely. Playing catch up has certainly made me work hard as there was always a chance of coming in in record time, even until a few days ago. I have never slacked off or I would always have been wondering if I could have actually done it. At least this way I know for sure I have fought hard until the end. There will always be the, what ifs- what if the weather has been better? What if I had left a week later? What if I had a lighter boat? What if I had gone further south early on? But, I can't change any of these things, my 46-day prediction was off the mark and I have lost my job as Mystic Meg's replacement!

As it stands I think I should get in on Monday or perhaps Sunday night if I get some good mileage in. This is an absolutely incredible time and I am extremely proud of myself. However, I still have a few days to go yet so I will write about that when the time comes.

Apart from my latest delivery I have hardly seen any shipping movement for a few weeks. Today I saw a yacht and a ship on the same course as me so I guess both are heading to one of the islands. Now I am closer to land I expect to see a few more boats and ships moving so will keep a good look out especially at night. Everything commercial and a lot of private boats will set my AIS alarm off, but there could be the odd private boat that won't so regular visual checks are essential.

The full moon last night was amazing, it just lights up everything. I got some pictures but they just don't do it justice. Not long to go now! "Oh, we're going to Barbados"

Day 46 0900hrs stats:

Past 24hr Distance 61nm

Total Distance 2440nm

Max Speed 4.35kts

Min speed 1.08kts

Avg speed 2.54kts

21st February 2019

Thoughts of home

Just 250nm left to go!!! Up until now I have not really thought much about finishing and getting home, I have tried to concentrate on the task in hand.

Now the end is in sight I have started to think about my lovely little house and can't wait to get back there. It is surrounded by trees, we have squirrels and all kinds of wildlife visit the garden and the river is just down the end of the road. I love it, especially on warm evenings when me and Jaime can sit on the deck and enjoy dinner with a glass of wine.

Jaime, Mum and Dad are all flying out to Barbados tomorrow, I can't wait to see them. That's going to be brilliant seeing their lovely faces. I wonder if it will be like when I left. As in... how long do you keep waving for!! From a vantage point they will probably be able to see me a few hours before I actually arrive. I am not sure where they will be, I am hoping that it will be daylight and pretty straight forward for them to find me.

Message from Mum:

Good morning my darling, we are so pleased you are feeling better! Hope conditions stay good for your final few days. All good at home see you soon, lots of love Mum and Dad.

I have my Barbados chart out and marked up ready to go. I have a waypoint marked up on the Northern point then I will follow the island round into Port Saint Charles. There seem to be a few reefs and obstructions to avoid but these are clearly marked up on the chart, plus I should have a boat coming out to escort me in. Feels exciting to start planning the arrival in my head now. Nearly there!!!!

It's been a pretty dreary day with a few patches of rain. The wind has been very strange, one minute it's blowing a hooley, the next its flat calm. This is caused by small areas of low pressure passing through, there is no point trying to navigate round them – I am just holding course and dealing with whatever the wind is doing hour by hour.

I wish I could catch these flying fish on camera for you, they are amazing to watch. A group of about fifteen all flew out of the water a few feet from the boat and in formation made a good 20metre flight before re-entering the water. I have noticed that as they begin to lose altitude, they swish their tail on the surface of the water to get a bit of momentum going again.

Plastic watch today – a big blue plastic bag floating just below the surface of the water, I could not be sure but it looked like it may have been tied at the top so probably contained more rubbish. Well that was my last Thursday sunset!! Here's hoping for a trouble free night and some good rowing conditions for the remainder of my crossing.

Thank you all again for following my journey and helping to spread awareness about the problem of plastics pollution in our oceans.

Day 47 0900hrs stats:

Past 24hr Distance 64nm

Total Distance 2504nm

Max Speed 6.01kts

Min speed 2.16kts

Avg speed 2.67kts

22nd February 2019

Digging in deep

Wow what a tough day!! Most days have been tough, but when you think it's all downhill from here and the weather chucks in another slow day.. it takes a lot of will power not to lose the plot!!!

Without a deadline to have to hit, I had planned on using the good weather forecast to enjoy the last few days by taking it down half a gear and clearing out the treats locker by eating it all. With 18kts of wind forecast this would mean only a minimal amount of lost time and I would come in to Barbados looking like I had just done a trip round the bay.

However, during the night last night the conditions slowed right up and at one point I was driving the oars as hard as I could and only making 1.3kts. Not only had the wind dropped but I also appeared to have a current hitting my starboard side creating waves that continuously rocked the boat from side to side making it virtually impossible to get any good purchase with the oars in the water.

To try and keep up some kind of mileage I have been on the oars for 12hrs almost non-stop, I have had a few 10-15min comfort breaks but apart from that it's been non-stop. I have set my mind on getting in Monday evening now, with the speeds today this 'could' delay to Tuesday morning and if these conditions continue it could roll on to Wednesday. This is why I can't now enjoy a nice leisurely row in, I have to keep pushing especially while the conditions are slow.

I messaged Charlie Pitcher (my amazing Yoda!) who says that the forecast shows the wind picking up again, but more importantly to stay strong as I have the whole way across. I am nearly there,

there will be set backs but I will get there. He also commended me on how strong I have been and how hard I have worked in the face of some very tough conditions. This means a lot to me coming from him as he is a seasoned Ocean rower with a few records under his belt. Needless to say I got back into fight mode and kept rowing.

Something else that has kept me going today is news from Zoë (my amazing sister in law who has been looking after my social media) she has told me about all the support I have got not just locally but across the world. Children from schools in different countries are doing projects on me, this is just amazing. I am looking forward to catching up with it all and thanking you all again. It has also got my brain working overdrive as to how to keep the momentum going, I certainly don't plan to end the campaign when I land. I have lots of great ideas in the pipeline so keep following Row Aurora to be in the know.

Its 10.30pm UK time and 5.30pm local Barbados time as I write this. The sun set about 20mins ago. My family should have landed in Barbados by now so I am the closest I have been to them for nearly two months. So so close!! I am pulling out all the stops to get there as soon as I possibly can.

Message from Paul:

Keep focused on what a massive difference you have made already and how many people have changed their ways because of your efforts. Also dont forget the serious bragging rights you will have earned when you rock up on dry land and complete your challenge. Keep going you legend. Almost there. Sheldrake.

The wind seems to have picked up very slightly now, I will still row during the night- but as I have done so many hours today I will be trying to get some well-earned rest in too.

As I seem to have done most days, I have my fingers crossed for better conditions tomorrow!!

Day 48 0900hrs stats:

Past 24hr Distance 61nm

Total Distance 2565nm

Max Speed 8.27kts

Min speed 2.71kts

Avg speed 2.54kts

23rd February 2019

7 weeks at sea today!!

It's letter day. I love this part of the week as I get to open Molly and Rosie's letter. This one was a fantastic drawing of me rowing across the finish line with congratulations messages. I am a bit sad this is my last letter, thank you girls this really was an important part of my journey.

The ocean is definitely making me work for this right up until the last knockings. There is still an adverse current against me which is making holding a course harder, rowing is about as tough as it gets, waves hitting the boat beam on soaking me every 20mins or so (I actually believe that the ocean deliberately waits until I am dry and have warmed up, or knows I was about to go in the cabin) these arduous conditions have of course effected my speed, which means I just cannot achieve the distance needed to get in on Monday now. Yet another day pushed back whilst my family are waiting patiently for me in Barbados. I can't even describe the feeling of watching the speed over ground display remain so slow knowing it's putting my arrival time further away yet again.

Message from Teresa Barr:

Hey, not long now, so proud of you. You are one hell of a woman, you know that dont you? What an amazing inspiring hero you are. Sooooooo close now. Cant wait to see you when you get back.

I am trying so hard to remain upbeat and enjoy these last few days, but these conditions are not making it easy. I really am not sure I would be holding it together still if I didn't know how many people are cheering me on. I also have brought a few reminders of home, cards and good luck charms with me that I look through on a regular basis to remind me to keep going.

key ring from Anya, Mason and Zac my beautiful niece and nephews, an angel from Sheila and Mary Ann, card and handwritten hymn from Jean Taylor (I will post the hymn when I get back its beautiful) I also have a St Christopher from Teresa, an angel from my mum and a compass from Chris Bird round my neck. Of course you have already met Bert the guardian angel toy doggie from my dad, I have a little chat with him every night.

I know will get there eventually and these testing times just make the success even more rewarding.

I have just spoken to Jaime via text in Barbados, he says a two man rowing boat just came in today. These two guys are South African and left the Canaries (different island to me) three days before me. They confirmed the strong swirling currents on the lead up to Barbados. I am not sure if it's a good or a bad thing I now know I have these conditions all the way in. I wonder what point they overtook? I hope they are still there when I arrive to swap some war stories! It will be interesting to see their route and if they got caught in the same weather systems as me. I bet they didn't get a beer delivery at half way!

I have had no music the past couple of days as it has again been quite thick cloud cover and my batteries need to be preserved for essential equipment. I got some reasonable sun this afternoon, but still not quite enough to get the batteries back to full strength. I will certainly appreciate things in life more when I get back. For example, we take for granted that you turn on the tap if you are thirsty, I have not been able to do that and many people on the planet have no access to clean water.

Well yet again the sun sets with me praying to anyone that will listen to give me some nice conditions for my last couple of days so that my arrival is not pushed back again. If you can all join me that would be very much appreciated. I have just 150nm left to go, COME ON ME!! I CAN DO THIS!!!

Day 49 0900hrs stats:

Past 24hr Distance 68nm

Total Distance 2633nm

Max Speed 6.01kts

Min speed 2.71kts

Avg speed 2.83kts

24th February 2019

Less than 100nm to go

Tuesday morning is my expected arrival time, although the conditions are finally spot on so I may have to actually slow down to avoid arriving in the middle of the night with nobody ready to see me in!!

I can't see any land yet, but after 3000miles less than 100 sounds closer than it actually is. I will definitely be singing a song when it comes in to view.

Today has been amazing conditions, if only it had been like this a bit sooner. A nice following wind, a few good waves and a nice bit of sun. It's been lovely to row in and I have even been able to get the boat in order ready for arrival in Barbados. There is still a side current trying to take me South, but I have been able to stay on course pretty well. However, I have still been caught by a few rogue waves, I gave up with hanging my towel out to dry in the end.

I can't believe tomorrow will be my last full day on the Ocean! It seems surreal that this row is coming to an end. I spent yesterday wishing the time away so I could get on dry land, but today I have been feeling sad it's nearly up. I am very keen to see my friends and family and get into a shower, (my friends and family will want me to get in a shower too I bet!!) but I have definitely got so much from this experience that I will be sad to leave it behind. I feel much more connected to the Ocean and have a new found respect for the wonder of everything connected to it. It's amazing that one day it can gently deliver a turtle to come visit me or silhouette dolphins so beautifully under the moonlight then the next have the strength to pick me and my whole boat up and hurtle it at nearly 15kts down a wave. The immense power of the ocean is something that deserves total respect, that's why it's so sad to see the negative effects the human race is having on it. Things are changing and I hope we can have a positive effect.

The only thing that could have put the icing on the cake for this would have been to see a whale. Maybe I will see one tomorrow?

I had a chat with Angus earlier who is sorting out my shore support, I am really made up he will be there to see me in. He will be with Jaime and a guy called Brian on board a fishing boat and we will arrange a waypoint to meet north of the island. As Brian is very experienced in the water around the island, they will be able to guide me round the safe passage into port. I have all the charts and planned my route in for myself just in case, but after rowing for over 50 days a 'follow me' boat is an exceptionally welcome end to the passage.

Message from Jaime:

Just met up with Angela and Alex who have flown out to wave you in. Have a meeting with Angus in 15mins to sort out what happens when you get to the Island. Love you baby xxxx

I am just settling in for what is my penultimate night at sea, I don't plan to row too hard and will ensure I get some rest. But, as ever I will be alert to check for other vessels and the boat systems are good. All is well aboard the good ship True Blue and the campaign of Row Aurora is due to be an incredibly successful mission.

Day 50 0900hrs stats:

Past 24hr Distance 71nm

Total Distance 2704nm

Max Speed 7.13kts

Min speed 2.16kts

Avg speed 2.96kts

25th February 2019

Crossing the line!!!

I have only gone and done it!!! I have rowed single handed the entire way across the Atlantic Ocean!! Absolutely wow!! As I type this I am sitting in my villa in Barbados, I have not had a chance to blog since the 24th so here goes with trying to remember the whirlwind which was the last few days!!

Day 51 0900hrs stats:

Past 24hr Distance 75nm

Total Distance 2779nm

Max Speed 7.13kts

Min speed 1.62kts

Avg speed 3.13kts

The conditions picked up nicely overnight and I decided to get a bit of a move on. So much so, I have now updated my arrival time from Tuesday morning to TONIGHT!! I have spoken to Angus from Rannoch who is organising the logistics of my arrival who has said this is amazing work, the only problem being the customs office closes at 10pm.

What this could mean is that I would not be permitted to go ashore, I would have to drop anchor or pick up a mooring outside the marina overnight and come ashore in the morning when the office opens. Not the end of the world, but a massive anti-climax.

So the race is now on to get in on time. At 0900 today my boat speed averaged 3kts which gives me an ETA at the top of the island of 9.30pm. This is cutting it really fine as there is still about 5 miles to go from the 'finish line' into port, so Angus is now also trying to organise a tow boat to get me down the west side of the island as quickly as possible.

The idea of a tow the last part does not sit well with me as it feels a little like cheating the last bit. Of course it isn't, and it's got to be a better option than sitting at anchor waving at the people on shore all night. I wholeheartedly trust whatever plans Angus makes and all I can do is row my socks off this last few hours to try and make it in on time.

The day is beautiful sunshine, reasonable winds and a bit of swell in the ocean giving me a nice row in (I love the choppy sea state) however, not long after confirming I could make the deadline if I kept up the pace, the currents moved round making the going quite tough again. I was able to almost keep up to 3kts (adrenaline is kicking in now) but gradually my ETA was slowly falling back. With nothing I could do but row, I just got stuck in, enjoyed my last day and trusted there would be a cunning plan to clear me through customs.

What a great day it was too, I took the opportunity to get some final photos on my breaks and made sure my boat was set up for landing. I think it was about 2pm Barbados time when land first came into view, it was just a misty silhouette at first, but land it definitely was. What an incredible moment, I stood up and looked over the bow of the boat for a few moments to take in the scene. Over fifty days since I last saw land and here is was again, beginning to appear over the horizon. I am sure if you check my tracker, you might even see the speed pick up as I get excited.

Time has gone relatively quickly over the past 7 weeks. Suddenly it was as if time was going backwards. I would row for what seemed like hours only to find out I had been going for twenty minutes. I was loving every second, but I did find it amusing that with land now in sight it seemed like this was the longest stretch. What was a fantastic motivator and also sped time up slightly was finding a radio station. The speaker I have been using also picks up FM radio. As I could see land I guessed the radio masts would be on the highest point, so decided to try and tune in. It was like finding civilisation and my first connection to the island what an absolutely brilliant moment. As I flicked through the channels there is was, Barbados Capital Radio playing some great music and giving me an insight into the news of the island that was now so close. Hearing voices for the first time was a great moment too, it put a great big smile on my face.

With some great music and the feeling of being connected to land again, I again found the energy to keep up the momentum. However, with the current slowing me down I now had an ETA of 10pm to the top of the island. This would mean missing customs and my window of getting ashore tonight. I decided there was nothing I could do but keep going and hope they would take pity on me and hold the office open. With my fingers and toes crossed I kept going (and singing.)

The sun was now beginning to set on my final day on the ocean. It was pretty emotional to know that when it had gone behind the horizon, the next time I saw it would be dry land. I downed oars for half an hour to watch the sun go down and drink the beer I had been saving for this moment since my chance meeting with SV Lola over two weeks ago.

As the sun completely set I was then met with the magical sight of the lights of the island. It's such a complete contrast to every other night, it took my breath away for a moment.

Back to the oars and an ETA check, still 10pm to the top of the island! With the additional 5miles to get ashore this was looking doubtful I would be on dry land tonight. But I could only keep going and hope for the best. I continued to row into the dark with the waves getting choppier the closer to land I got.

I must have been hit by about five flying fish. The whole crossing without one, and now they were coming out in force. They glistened in the light from my navigation lights so I could see them coming but was not able to move out of the way quick enough for a few of them.

9.45pm and I am just a mile and a half from the line when I am joined by three motor boats. One with crew from the Barbados Rotary, the Marine Police unit, and the third with Angus on board to help guide me in.

I was overwhelmed that all these people had come out to sea at night in these conditions just to ensure my safe passage to port.

The conditions were now not ideal, there were heavy rain downpours and the sea state meant that if I was in the trough of a wave I could not see the navigation lights of the other boats and they could not see me. I have hundreds of hours of sea time during darkness, but after being the only boat for miles around for over 7 weeks I was actually getting a bit nervous.

I was in radio contact with Angus who gave me some great news, customs had agreed to stay open until midnight. This was actually happening, I was just a few hours from dry land and just half hour from completing the most incredible task I had ever set myself.

At 10.15pm the radio crackled back into life "True Blue, this is Angus. Congratulations, you have just successfully rowed single handed and unsupported across the Atlantic Ocean." Over the sound of the wind and crashing waves I could then hear the crew from all three boats cheering. The feeling was amazing, I could not believe I had actually done it and it was over.

This feeling was very short lived as I now had the pretty dangerous task of setting up a tow and getting into port. I knew once we were round the west side of the island it would be sheltered, but in these conditions the first part of the tow would need some seriously good seamanship from both the towing vessel and myself. It would also be slow and careful going until getting into shelter, so we were still against the clock to get in for midnight.

I set about connecting my tow line to the front of the boat and checked it at least 5 times to make sure I got it right. I was pretty tired and did not want to make any mistakes. If the line was not clear to run through it could potentially pull the boat sideways swamping it and throwing me overboard, or would just rip off any piece of equipment it was caught on like the light mast or, worse still, a piece of me!!

Angus then came along side for me to throw the line to. This is a DANGEROUS manoeuvre. If the motorboat caught a wave it could get picked up and ploughed straight into the back of me, we really needed to get this right first time. As the boat closed in alongside I threw the line and it was about to land just short when Angus seemed to develop bionic stretching arms and somehow got it and we began the tow. This process had taken 30mins so we now had an hour and fifteen mins to get to customs. At a maximum safe tow speed of 5kts this was going to take about an hour giving just fifteen minutes leeway! The clock is ticking!!!

You may think once under tow I could kick back and relax but this was very far from the truth. I had to be fully alert and ready with the hand steering. If a wave picked me up I could now end up being ploughed into the back of the towing vessel. So I had to have steer for the duration of the tow and of course the rain came down again for another 15min burst.

11.40pm we arrive at the entrance to the marina where the tow line is disconnected and packed away. My last job is to row in and get on land. As it transpired the route in and berthing position could not have been any easier, it was extremely straight forward. However, in the dark with no local knowledge or experience getting into this marina and of course I am facing backwards I was a bit apprehensive about it.

Angus has now got ashore and called out "just go round that big blue boat and you will see everyone stood next to the pontoon you need to go to." I looked around expecting a 50 or 60ft boat... nothing? "I can't see a big blue boat" "it's the only one there, right in front of you." I looked round again and really could not work out where this boat was.

Then suddenly a lightbulb moment. When he said big he meant BIG!! There was a massive super yacht right in front of me "ohhhhh, THAT big blue boat!!"

So round I went to be greeted by not one or two, but a crowd of people cheering and waving flags and calling out support. I was totally overwhelmed, this was absolutely unexpected. 11.50pm I tied up on the pontoon to be greeted by Jaime and my parents. For once in my life I didn't really know what to say – it was like being a rabbit caught in headlights.

I went into the cabin to get my passport (11.55pm) and got off the boat to an amazing reception, there were camera crews from the TV station, photos, friends from home, people on holiday who had heard about what I was doing and came to greet me, the local rotary club, the minister for sport. I made my way through the crowd to customs (held up by my mum and dad as walking was not an easy task) hugging as many people as possible on the way through.

As the clock read 11.59pm I stepped into the customs office, I had made it with literally seconds to go. The customs officials were brilliant and I could not thank them enough for staying open late for me. All the paperwork was ready for me, I just had to check and sign it and I had officially arrived on the island.

Back out to the crowd and I began to meet and chat with everyone and thank them all for being there. I just could not believe the support I was being shown. I really felt like a celebrity posing for photos and being interviewed on camera. What a wonderful greeting and such a surprise.

So when I told you a few weeks ago about the Row Aurora HQ control room being set up by my parents this is part of what they had been organising. I could not have wished for a better arrival party.

After a couple of hours thanking everyone and sharing a few stories we went back to the villa we are staying in until Sunday when we fly home.

Sleeping in a bed without having to get up to row in a couple of hours will be bliss.

I have a busy day tomorrow cleaning the boat ready for shipping, then I have lots of appointments through the week which I will update you on in later blogs.

Thank you for reading I hope you have enjoyed my journey. Stay tuned as there are blogs coming from my adventures in Barbados.

Day 51 17hrs and 15mins @ 0215hrs GMT stats:

Past 17hrs 15min Distance 51nm

Total Distance 2830nm

Max Speed 6.57kts

Min speed 1.08kts

Avg speed 2.97`kts

OVERALL STATS:

Total distance 2830nm

3255statute miles

Max Speed 19.1kts 22mph

Min Speed 0kts 0mph

Average speed 2.28kts 2.62mph

26th February 2019

First day on dry land

I got a good 5 hours last night but I was awake quite early and could not get back to sleep. Everything feels quite strange, laying on a bed that's not moving for a start is pretty weird. It was nice to not have to worry about checking systems or emptying fish out of the foot well, I just lay there awake for an hour or so trying to take it all in.

My first job of the day was an interview with the BBC via FaceTime. It is due to go out later today on local news but I understand it also made national news. I really want to get onto the morning slot of my local radio station at home Heart SX, but as I am 4hrs behind we keep missing each other. I am sure we will catch up when I get back but in the meantime I have sent some voice clips for the news.

I have not logged in to social media or emails yet as I want to give it my full attention and I have so much here yet to do. I have been passed a lot of it from Jaime and Zoë though, I just cannot comprehend the level of support you have all shown me. It's really emotional and made the whole thing a million times more important to me. That's why I want to sit for a couple of days and read it all properly rather than just flicking through.

Next task down to the boat and give it a good scrub out. If it gets packed into the shipping container with anything that's damp or likely to go mouldy that will be a disgusting job cleaning up back in the UK.

It was great going back to the yacht club in the daylight, I could now appreciate what a beautiful place this was. It took a good few hours to take everything off and get it in order. About 4pm we packed the car with some things to take back to the villa to dry out or put in the washing machine, with the plan of getting it all sorted and back to the boat before sunset, leaving tomorrow daytime free to explore the island. That was not to be….

We pulled into a petrol station to fill up. They have attendants here, so she asked how much we wanted and started filling up for us. All done she came back to the window and said "it was petrol you wanted?" "Erm, no, this is a diesel car."

We now had a tank of premium unleaded in our lovely diesel hire car!!!!! As Jaime is a mechanic he knows full well that many people do this to their own cars, let alone someone else's, so this was just a mistake and no point getting annoyed about. The garage called the local mechanic who came out and drained the tank getting us back on the road. Whilst the mechanic was working, I was chatting to the (I am guessing manager or supervisor) lady making the calls. She asked if we were on holiday, and when I told her I had rowed here she was really excited and said she had read all about me in the newspaper. I am quite the local celebrity now! It's just so surreal!

By the time we got back to our villa it was 7pm, so I got washed and cleaned what I needed, and would have to return to the boat tomorrow to finish the job.

An early night for another day of not yet relaxing tomorrow.

Just to update you on how I am coping being on land, I am amazed at how good I feel. A bit of a back ache in the morning but other than that I have no land sickness or aches and pains. I can walk fine and feel great. My calf muscles need building back up, but they are not painful at all. Angus says it's because I looked after myself so well at sea that it is paying off now.

27th February 2019

More housework

Up and out by 10am this morning with all the kit I had brought back to clean and dry to go back on the boat.

Whilst down at the yacht club doing the last of the packing I had quite a few people coming over to find out about me and my strange looking little boat. People love to hear about the adventure I have just had and it makes it all more real for people to picture what I am talking about when they can see me with my boat.

The last job is to clean through the water maker. As the pump now has sea water sitting in it, if I leave it the water will go off and damage the filter. This involves disconnecting the inlet hose so it is no longer taking water from the sea and placing the hose into a bucket of water with a treatment chemical in it. The pump is then run, cleaning it out and leaving the treatment solution inside.

As a professional mariner I am very pleased with my last couple of days work getting the boat in order. If you look after your boat she will look after you. True Blue has kept me safe for the last seven weeks, its only right she should now get the full spa treatment.

The afternoon brings more media coverage. I could get used to this!! I was speaking live to Dave Monk on BBC Essex. It was really great to speak to him as we did an interview back in July, so to be able to give an update about my successful crossing was great. We are making arrangements for me to go into the studio when I get back. You will all get bored of the sight and sound of me soon!

Tonight I have been invited at the request of the Minister for Tourism to an event at the incredible Lancaster Great House. This was built in the 1600s and is breath-taking.

As we arrived we were announced by a man in period costume which was very similar to a town crier. Walking up the huge staircase was like going back in time with beautiful old paintings on the walls and stunning furniture in every room.

Outside, the grounds were lit with fairy lights and set up ready for the live music to start later in the evening. The purpose of the event was to celebrate Tourism on the island by thanking people who have contributed to the industry, including people born here, people who have moved to the island and people who visit.

I was very honoured to firstly be invited and then to receive a special mention during the speeches. This was a very special night with many important people attending, and speaking to everyone made me feel very welcome indeed.

More TV interviews and more arrangements for the next few days – I am beginning to think I should have stayed an extra few weeks to fit it all in. This is a very special island with very special people. I will definitely be back again, but I might fly next time like most people do.

I have a bit of a reputation back home of getting up on stage whenever we are out. Tonight was no exception!!!! The band very very kindly let me join them for a song. I sang Mustang Sally, however the band had never heard it before. They were such incredible musicians that they said just start singing and we will join in. It went down a storm!! I am sure there is video evidence I can share with you when I get home.

After a great night of dancing and singing it's off to sleep ready for another packed day of invitations to more events and meetings tomorrow.

28th February 2019

The amazing Rotary Club

Today I was invited to the Barbados Rotary lunch as the guest speaker. I was so honoured to have been invited and it was a privilege to be able to speak to everyone.

It does seem a bit surreal that little old me would have anything inspiring to say, I am just an ordinary person. I suppose that is what makes it so special, showing that ordinary people can do extraordinary things. I am no athlete, I am not a natural academic, I am just someone who set a goal born from a dream and worked extremely hard to achieve it. Of course I don't expect everyone to go out and row the Atlantic, but to find their own dream and strive to make it come true.

The Rotary club have been incredible since my dad contacted them a couple of months ago. They formed a huge part of my arrival party, making me feel so very welcome and ensuring that we are being looked after during our stay in Barbados. The least I could do was to speak at their lunch.

I have also been interviewed for the Barbados newspapers this morning, I will have to try and get clippings and recordings of all the media I have had out here. It's crazy, everyone knows me and even if they don't recognise me they have heard my story. I am just can't believe the coverage I am getting.

After lunch it's off to the next official engagement, meeting the deputy chief of police on the island. The police marine patrol boat had been part of the escort into port, it was an extremely comforting sight to see the blue lights following as part of the fleet.

Whilst speaking with the command team they were overwhelmed by what I had done and were disappointed I was not a member of the Barbados police. They would have used me as part of their recruitment campaign to attract and inspire women to the job.

I had visions of getting off the boat, nobody knowing who I was and spending the week on the beach. Instead I have been non-stop, it's been an absolute whirlwind. I would not change it for the world though, it's so great to be able to give something back to everyone who have made me feel so welcome. It's also a good excuse to come back and visit again to enjoy the beautiful beaches and visit even more of the island.

Another busy but wonderful day, I have made so many friends that will be with me forever.

1st March 2019

Party central

Wow the 1st of March!! It was the day after Boxing Day when I was last at home! Now it's the first of March and I am on an incredible island feeling like a celebrity after rowing across the Atlantic Ocean for seven weeks!! It's going to be very strange going home.

My first engagement this morning was speaking with Vic Fernandes, chairman and morning presenter at Capital Media Barbados radio.

This was a brilliant live on air interview. It was so great to be in the studio with the team who gave me my first connection to the island.

If you remember my blog from when I was on my last day rowing, I was able to connect to a radio station from 2pm until midnight. These were the first voices I had heard for seven weeks apart from a few VHF radio messages, it was a real uplifting moment. It was, of course, Capital Media and what a coincidence that I then met Vic who invited me on to the show.

After that it was on patrol with the Police Marine section. It was quite funny that the guys have an almost identical job to me, but they get to do it on a Caribbean island! I could be tempted to transfer, but don't tell my boss!

The afternoon took us to lunch with John and Rain Chandler at Limegrove. What an incredible afternoon at an amazing restaurant. John and Rain own Lancaster house where we had been guests of the minister for tourism on Wednesday night.

Lancaster house is full of beautiful antiques as is their restaurant. There are all sorts of interesting pieces. It's a shame we are not staying longer so we could have experienced a party night as there is also two full racks of period costumes, dresses fit for Hollywood and carnival headdresses. I can imagine this being a pretty outrageous night out.

John used to own a hotel on the island so has some incredible stories about celebrities who have stayed with him over the years, I am just reading his book on it all. We can't thank them enough for their kind hospitality, I would recommend a visit to the restaurant if you are ever on the island, beautiful food, friendly staff and great surroundings.

With conversation and Martinis in full flow, lunch did not finish until 7pm, and it was straight out across the road to attend the 3 year anniversary party for Capital Media. I feel like a local now, attending parties where I know people.

The final stop of the day was at a pub to meet our friends Angela and Alex who had flown out especially to see me in. It was wonderful to catch up with them to swap stories. It's been great to hear things from the other side.

Whilst I was rowing in I had no concept of what was going on or what information was getting through. Just wonderful to hear it all from the other side and see the pictures. I am not sure I will ever get to hear everyone's experiences and put the whole picture together, but I am going to try my best and really enjoy doing it.

2nd March 2019

A day at the races

Our last full day on the island, and what a day it turned out to be.

The first stop was at the model UN conference. This is an event for some incredible young people. This morning was practice and feedback for the main event, each person represented a country and spoke on their behalf.

Each speech outlined details of the country, what they are doing to tackle a global problem and a call to the other countries to join them.

What an incredible group of young people, listening to them speak and support each other, I am sure there will be a few future political leaders in that room.

I spoke to them about my journey, not just the row itself but how hard I had worked to get there and why I have a passion for protecting our oceans. It was an honour to be able to inspire young people of Barbados and give a little back for the warm reception I have had here.

In the afternoon we were official guests of Mr John King, Minister for Sport at the Gold Cup. This is like Ascot with a Caribbean twist.

He had made a special effort to meet me on the night I rowed in to port and now I am his guest in the VIP area. Champagne and a beautiful buffet meant we were sure not to be hungry or thirsty all day. Rubbing shoulders with some very important people all day made me feel very special especially as they all wanted to meet and speak to me.

I am expecting the same treatment back in the UK of course!!! I will only attend events where I get free champagne and salmon buffet!

I don't know much about betting so I did not bet on any of the horses, I just enjoyed the atmosphere and sheer spectacle of the whole event. It seems that the whole island came out for what is the biggest event of the year. People from all around enjoy the carnival atmosphere. I was honoured to be there. I just keep pinching myself that this is all real.

Our flight home tomorrow is at 8pm, so we are hoping to get at least one tourist attraction in. I will let you know in tomorrow's blog if we managed it.

3rd March 2019

Going underground

I am excited about getting home and seeing my friends but will be really sad to leave this amazing island. I will be back for a holiday one day, I might even get to sit on one of the beautiful beaches.

We had to be out of the villa by 11am so we packed up and said goodbye to the place we had called home for the past week.

We then got to be tourists for the first time!!!! We went with our friends Jan, John Angela and Alex to Harrison's Cave. This is an underground cavern located in the centre of Barbados full of stalactites, stalagmites, cascading waterfalls, and natural passages. It's one of the island's top attractions, and rightly so— it's incredible. Apparently Barbados is the only Caribbean Island which was not formed by volcano activity. It's actually formed by the earth's plates. Don't say you didn't learn anything from this book!!!

After a lovely day it was off to the Airport for the final leg of this epic adventure. When checking in I tried to explain what I had done to blag an upgrade... it did not work. In fact the lady behind the check in desk did not seem very impressed by my story. She either did not believe me or did not get what I was saying. I don't mind airports and travelling, but on the way out to your destination it's all exciting and part of the trip. On the way back I just want to be able to click my fingers and be home, everything seems to drag and just be hard work.

Needless to say I did treat myself in one of the jewellery shops with a Barbados charm for my bracelet. Well, actually, I could not decide which one so I bought two! We boarded without incident and got ready for the flight. I must have been tired as I did not even watch a whole film. Before I knew it, we were landing!

4th March 2019

Back on UK soil

Well the flight went pretty quick as I am sure I slept through most of it. Nothing really to report, we got our bags in one piece and I started to think about what was in store. Would it be back to normal like nothing happened? Will I feel differently about life? Will life ever really be the same?

Whilst walking towards the exit doors pulling my suitcase behind me, my thoughts continued to swim around my head. What I was not expecting was a lone female stood right in front of the doors holding up a piece of cardboard with the writing "I love you Dawn Wood, you are my hero"

I have to be honest she looked pretty sad and lonely all on her own like some crazy stalker. I was prepared for the odd person from my town to recognise me, but I did not think my celebrity status had reached crazy stalker fan level!! I could not very well ignore her firstly as I was now pretty much stood right in front of her. Secondly, I felt a little sorry for her I imagined she had travelled some distance to see me in all on her own so I really wanted to give her a hug and thank her for her support. As I took a step closer and went in for the hug, I noticed a crowd of friends from my home town Burnham on Crouch all waving banners and flags. My first thought was that I wanted to see my friends, but I could not ignore this lady. Then I started to smell a rat!!

It transpired that this lone lady is actually my friends new girlfriend so had come along with all my mates. As I had never met her before I did not recognise her, they got me hook line and sinker!! I must admit I was a little disappointed that I had not actually got a crazy stalker lady, but, I soon got over it when I got to hug all my mates. I could not believe everyone had come out so early in the morning to see me in. It was a wonderful surprise and such a great moment to see all their lovely smiling faces.

I had plans to spend the day sorting through my mountains of admin, emails and messages but as soon as we got home I pretty much straight away fell asleep on the sofa. That's where I stayed for the rest of the day getting up only to eat pizza and go to the loo (in the toilet not a bucket!!)

March 2019

The whirlwind continues!

In answer to my previous question, will it go back to normal when I get home? The answer is NO!! It's been an absolute whirlwind with more media appointments, school visits, talks and project development ideas.

The day after getting home I was filming with ITV on the river front at the Royal Burnham Yacht Club. This was my first glimpse of the river I had spent so many hours training on since leaving over two months ago. It looked pretty calm out there to me now after what I had just experienced. I took a good long deep breath and internally thanked the river for being a massive part of my life.

The day after that I was in the studio at Sky, I feel like a bit of a pro at this TV lark now- I think I could do some presenting of my own one day ha ha.

The next day on air with Martin, Su and Alex from Heart SX, the gang have been amazing. Whilst I have been away they have followed me and kept the listeners up to date with my journey, on this day I got so much airtime and really boosted my fundraising profile (I am up to about 12K for the marine conservation society now!). Thank you to the morning crew.

On to Friday and international Women's Day, I have been invited to talk at an event in Chelmsford. The event is set up by representatives of the police, fire and ambulance and is aimed at inspiring women in the emergency services. It was a fantastic day meeting lots of people who had inspiring stories of their own. I was sitting at one of the tables listening to the guest speakers whilst merrily filling my face with the complimentary chocolates, when I suddenly realised my picture was up on the screen. The

Chief Constable of Essex went on to talk about me and my achievements, I was sure that I was going to be called up on stage, so I had to chew and swallow everything I had in my gob as quickly as possible! Sure enough I was called on stage and to my surprise I was awarded a chief constables commendation for outstanding achievement. I was very proud to have been awarded this, and to have not had chocolate on my teeth in the photos!

Before I knew it and without a moments rest, I was back at work. First task of my first day back...attend a meeting, but it was not all bad as the boss had brought in cakes!!

My home coming party was an incredible evening. It is the first thing related to my Row that I had absolutely no part in organising. My wonderful husband Jaime booked a fantastic band who had agreed I could join them for a few songs (I hope i did not outstay my welcome on stage!!) My fantastic friends also did an amazing job in helping setting up with decorations and inviting everyone. It felt a bit like a wedding as I wanted to get round to everyone to say thank you but i just did not get round to everyone. A massive heart felt thank you to everyone who came along.

Since being back in the UK I have attended many local schools telling them about not only my row, but spreading the message about plastic pollution and inspiring young people. The children never fail to amaze me with their enthusiasm for the subject, they all know not to drop rubbish and the effect our plastic pollution is having on the oceans and the world we live in. I have had a number of messages from parents and teachers telling me how my story has inspired change and made a real difference. Its messages like this that make the whole thing worthwhile.

I love the questions primary school children ask, most are better than the ones adults ask. (However, the one my friend got asked at a different talk will take a lot of beating. He was the police school liaison officer and was doing a stranger danger type talk. When he asked if there were any questions a sweet little girls asked "Why does my dog smell my cat's bottom?" I am not sure what answer he gave but I should imagine the leaving assembly music went on pretty quickly.) As well as school visits I have also been talking at locals groups and clubs spreading the word. It really is non-stop as it's not just the time taken to travel to the venue and deliver the talk, its preparing presentations and dealing with all the admin enquiries. I love it, but I do need to make sure I don't overdo things. I have a full time job on top of the Row Aurora campaign, so time management is key.

I was absolutely overwhelmed (I probably have used these words way too much lately!!) to receive an award from the Burnham Town Council for outstanding achievements. It's an absolutely beautiful trophy in the shape of a rower. I was so taken aback to have got this, but am so proud to have represented my beautiful town and hopefully made a difference in my community. My latest project is to get my town awarded plastic free status. I will be working on this over the next year and hope to make this a reality soon.

To the future

What's next?

Who knows what the future holds? I certainly intend to continue my work reducing single use plastics and encouraging others to do the same. I would also like to develop a role as an inspirational speaker. I want people to see that no matter who you are, where you come from, your abilities or disabilities there is something within you that you can excel in. It can be hard work striving for your goals but the tougher the journey the more rewarding it is when you get there. I am sure there will be an announcement soon as to my next big adventure, but for now I will be spending the next year working on my plastic free project and helping to train future ocean rowers.

I hope you have enjoyed reading my book, I have certainly enjoyed sharing my journey with you.

If you are down with the kids and use social media, please give me a follow and if you enjoyed reading this share your thoughts with me.

Thank you again to everyone who has been part of my journey. Without you this would never have happened.

Messages to Dawn

Overwhelming support

I received so many messages of support for people across the world. I wanted to share some of them with you here.

THE START OF THE LINK WITH BARBADOS

TO BARBADOS ROTARY CLUB 10 DEC 2018

Hi from Essex England! We're supporting a local lass (Dawn Wood) in her endeavours to highlight the problems associated with discarded plastic accumulating in our oceans, which is adversely affecting the marine ecosystem. Dawn is a police officer attached to the Essex Police Marine Section here in the United Kingdom and is passionate about the quality of the sea water locally and elsewhere in the world. She is currently visiting local schools to encourage the youngsters to 'be plastic smart' and contacting local businesses to take the challenge to reduce the reliance on 'single use' plastic.

To emphasise the devastating effect discarded plastic material is having on our world's oceans she plans to row solo and unsupported across the Atlantic Ocean from Gran Canaria to finish in your beautiful island of Barbados a distance of 3,000 miles. During the epic journey she will be carrying out sea water sampling for micro plastics, data collected will be made available for future investigation. Dawn will be leaving Gran Canaria around the 3rd or 4th January 2019 depending on weather conditions and 'hopes' to be arriving in Port St Charles, Barbados mid-February 2019. As we will be tracking her journey a more accurate date will be available nearer the time.

As mentioned, she is a serving UK police office and we understand contact has already be been made with the Royal Barbados Police to let them know Dawn will be on their patch in the new year! Is this initiative something you would be happy to support & perhaps publicise through the Barbados Rotary Club?

Many thanks for any assistance you're able to offer.

FROM THE ROTARY CLUB OF BARBADOS 11 DEC 2018

Thanks for your email.

As Secretary of the Rotary Club of Barbados, I have shared your email with our President, our Public Relations Director and our International Service Director. Also copied on this email is a long-standing member of our club and a past District 7030 Governor, who knows Port St. Charles and the local boating community very well.

Our club will be pleased to support Dawn and assist in publicizing this worthy mission. We extend an invitation to her to visit our club when she does arrive on island. Are you aware of any plans for a welcome event upon Dawn's arrival to Barbados?

Please continue to update this group on the mission and provide information which we can share within our club and in Barbados.

Club Secretary

The Rotary Club of Barbados

FEBRUARY 26, 2019 TO: JAIME WOOD; BARRY SMITH

Once again on behalf of the Rotary Club of Barbados, we congratulate Dawn and your family for a very successful completion of her mission. In spite of her arrival in the dead of night, Dawn's inner light shinned bright over us all, as we are all very inspired by her resilience and amazing spirit.

We cannot wait to see the four of you again on Thursday at our Rotary Club meeting. As a reminder we start promptly at 12:30pm so I suggest you arrive 15 to 20 minutes early to meet Rotarians and settle in before the meeting commences. Location is the Barbados Hilton. It should take you no more than 40 to 45 minutes from your villa with traffic. Are you using a GPS or perhaps Google maps? It will take you straight to the Hilton. Your Row Aurora polo shirts are perfect to wear.

26 FEB 2019, TO BARBADOS ROTARY: Many thanks for your congratulations – very much appreciated We are delighted with Dawn's recovery rate; she seems to be back to normal (whatever that might be!!!) Thanks again for your very kind invitation to the Rotary Club of Barbados lunch. We will be at the Hilton by about 1200 noon –with our row aurora tee shirts!! Look forward to seeing everyone again.

Regards Barry

TO SAILING VESSEL LOLA We are immensely grateful to you for taking the trouble to respond, as I said in the Instagram note 'thank you' seemed such an insignificant way of expressing our gratitude for what you did for our 'little girl'. Dawn informed us that she really savoured the oranges not having had any fresh fruit for many days. However, she enjoyed the chocolate more or less straight away – apparently to keep up her energy levels up and stop it melting! The events surrounding Dawn's Challenge of rowing across the Atlantic Ocean have been quite emotional, but your encounter was rather special because of your very kind gesture. We are pleased to hear you found Dawn well and in goods spirts. She is an Essex Police Officer attached to the Police Marine Unit, anything to do with the water, she is in her element. The previous vessel encounter during her crossing was the Cruise Liner the Queen Elizbeth, Dawn hailed the bridge and they acknowledge to say they had her on their AIS. They wished her a safe passage and Dawn responded likewise. No oranges, cheese, chocolate or beer though!!! Dawn should (fingers crossed) make land fall around the 23rd February give or take a couple of days. Her colleagues in the Essex Police have arranged for the Barbados Police to meet her when she arrives in their area of jurisdiction and escort her into Port St Charles. We have also been in touch with the Rotary Club of Barbados who are looking after Dawn's publicity on the Island and arranging a welcome for her when she arrives. Dawn's husband, Jaime would also like to pass on his grateful thanks to you for ensuring Dawn was safe and well before continuing your voyage and like us is very grateful to you for responding as you did. We are going the meet Dawn when she arrives in Barbados – I now know the words to the song "Woh I'm Going to Barbados" very well!!!! We wish you fair winds and a following tide for your voyages in your very impressive SV Lola. Kind regards Sheila & Barry,

FROM SV LOLA

Thanks so much for your note. We are delighted that you got in touch! We felt so lucky that our path and Dawn's passed close enough that we were able to see her AIS signal. When we first saw the signal, it was weak, so we could only see the speed, which made us worry it might be a boat in trouble. We called on the radio, but after failing to make contact, we diverted our course to investigate. As we drew nearer, and the AIS signal became stronger, the name and size of the boat were displayed, which really got our attention: True Blue seemed a very small boat to be mid-Atlantic. It wasn't until we were quite close, but not yet within visual range, that we were able to raise Dawn on the radio and when True Blue finally came into view, we were profoundly impressed by how tiny it looked as it disappeared and reappeared among the ocean swells. Over the radio Dawn sounded fantastic, cheerful and smiling. We worried we were being annoying by coming so close to her boat – all excited about our idea of attempting to transfer a goody bag to her – but she seemed game and when at last she was able to grab the line and pull the bag aboard True Blue, all of us were cheering a whooping in the cockpit of our boat. We lingered briefly after that, chatting a little with Dawn on the radio, but then it was time to go. We all wished each other safe voyages, and before we knew it, Dawn's boat had disappeared once more from our view, hidden in the Atlantic swell. Since then, Dawn has been front-and-centre in our thoughts and we have wondered about her experiences rowing True Blue across the wilderness of the Atlantic for so many days and nights.

For us the encounter with Dawn was a very special, "goose bumps" event. She looked great, tanned and strong, at home in her boat and in her element. Our daughter, who sent us your note via sat phone and who has relayed this reply to you, gave us more information about Dawn's voyage and we are completely awestruck by her undertaking and her bravery. You must be so very proud of your daughter an at the same time eager for her safe arrival in Barbados. I cannot know how I would feel if one of my children embarked on such a voyage, but I imagine it would be a mixture of giddy excitement, parental pride and abject terror. Maybe not unlike the way families of astronauts have felt. Anyway, Dawn continues to be very much in our thoughts as we approach Martinique, where we will make landfall in a few days. From there we will follow Dawn's progress towards Barbados with keen interest. Our brief encounter with your daughter made our first trans-Atlantic voyage very, very special indeed. All our best wishes, 300 miles east of Martinique aboard our boat Lola.

P.S. We would be happy to share the photos we took. Just let us know if you'd like us to email them or share them on another way via the internet

TO SV LOLA FROM DAWN

Hope everything is well with you. I'm just getting back to what is called normality after being in a small row boat for 51 days 17 hours and 15 minutes. I felt I had to contact you personally to thank you so much for your generosity and concern about a fellow mariner. The fresh fruit you gave me was something I could not have even dreamt about after so long at sea and living on dehydrated food. I arrived at the 'North Point' in Barbados the finish of my Challenge at 22.15 hrs (local time) and found that if I didn't get to the Customs Office in Port St Charles before it closed, I may end up having to stay on 'True Blue' until the following morning when the Customs Office opened again. The Barbados officials were excellent and needless to say I arrived and registered my documents on time. I was met by my lovely family, friends and many other people including the Barbados Minister of Sport at midnight - no less. I was so taken aback I was lost for words ...which isn't like me!! I will always remember my encounter with your wonderful family and the amazing Lola, she was a magnificent sight coming towards me in the vast expanse of the Atlantic Ocean. My family were also very appreciative about what you did for me and you will forever be in our thoughts when we recall events of my epic Challenge. May you have fair winds and a following tide for the rest of your voyage.

My very best wishes, I shall always remember you with great affection.

Dawny

TO SAILING VESSEL ORINOCO 21ST FEBRUARY 2019

Hi to the wonderful crew of the Orinoco,

May I thank you most sincerely for what you did recently for our 'little girl' Dawn Wood, who is rowing from Gran Canara to Barbados to highlight the problem of plastic pollution in our oceans. She is now on the final stage of her 3,000-mile Challenge and your wonderful gesture has certainly brought the smile back on her face and we can actually see this via your website. May we copy the superb photos you have displayed on your website? Vielen Dank, may your continued voyage be safe and enjoyable.

Kind regards Dawn's husband Jaime and Barry & Sheila (Dawn's parents)

Row Aurora Essex England UK.

FROM: SV ORINOCO DATE: TUE, 2 APR 2019

TO DAWN

Thank you very much, Dawn, for your mail. I am so glad to find you well! Even if our crossing from Tenerife to Grenada via Barbados only lasted four weeks, and was almost nothing compared to your adventure, I also needed some time to reorganize myself (having a job as university teacher and researcher). Now it is so good to hear from you again. Orinoco crew thinks a lot about you. We regret to have been so stunned, unsure how to behave, and nearly speechless when we met you in the middle of the ocean. Only later did we fully realize that we had an encounter nobody would ever forget in his life. Best regards from Hannover. Uwe

FROM: CAROL SENT: 06 APRIL 2019 RE: DAWN

Dawn deserves a big pat on the back for the service she has given to humanity not to mention the sea creatures. You must be so proud of her achievement and bravery to row all that way across terrible seas, alone and to do it in that time. Exceptional. Well done Dawn. I'm sure she should have had more media coverage. I'm so glad she is safely back home. Best regards Carol

BBC BREAKFAST TV PROGRAMME:

We have been contacted by numerous people (residents of Essex) commenting on a recent (17/12/18) BBC Breakfast programme feature Dawn Wood (Row Aurora). Dawn is shortly setting off to fly to Gran Canaria to start a monumental solo crossing of the Atlantic to highlight plastic pollution in our oceans. She will end her Challenge in Barbados (Port St Charles) – the Royal Barbados Police and the Island's Rotary Club have been informed of her proposed date of arrival and they, along with others have agreed to give her a very warm welcome to their lovely Island. Best Wishes for Christmas & the New Year

Kind regards

TO RAIN & JOHN (BARBADOS) 02 MARCH 2019 :

Hi Rain & John,

Just a short message to say a BIG thank you for your wonderful hospitality and the excellent meal – it was very much appreciated. We felt honoured to be invited to your restaurant and to be in your company. Hopefully, we will return to your lovely Island in the future and who knows we may meet up again – we certainly hope so!!

Best wishes on behalf of Dawn (Atlantic Rower) Jaime, Sheila & Barry

FROM: RAIN CHANDLER SENT: 03 MARCH 2019

It was so lovely to meet you all and to spend a little time with you. What Dawn has done is truly amazing and I know that there has to be wonderful people supporting most great achievements so congratulations to you all as a family. We would love to stay in touch and hope to see you in Barbados again. It really was a pleasure meeting you all. very best wishes Rain.

THANK YOU, TO THE ROTARY CLUB OF BARBADOS

5TH MARCH 2019 TO ROTARY CLUB OF BARBADOS

We have arrived home safely – however, just as we started to acclimatise to the hot Barbados weather, we are now facing 10 °C in Essex.

As I have said on numerous occasions – without the invaluable support of Rotary Club of Barbados, Dawn's visit would not have run as smoothly as it did. She certainly would not have met such inspirational and special Barbadians as she did – truly a remarkable country & people! Hopefully, for Dawn this is not the end of her mission but merely the start of an international campaign to reduce plastic pollution in our oceans and the reliance on single use plastic. We in turn wish you every success with your own campaign to improve the environment.

Our everlasting gratitude to everyone at Rotary for your welcome and assistance, we will never forget our new friends.

Best regards on behalf of Team Dawn....... Dawn, Jaime, Sheila & Barry.

MARCH 2019 FROM ROTARY CLUB OF BARBADOS

We thank Momma Smith and you for giving the world your daughter for 52 days. It was an honour to have been even a small part of what was an amazing journey, one that will live with us forever. You have raised a truly beautiful, inspirational (even if a tad crazy) woman. Nothing would make me prouder for my two daughters to grow up into someone like her.

We hope to see our Queen of the Ocean again in the near future. Until then Godspeed to you and your family.

YIR Adrian

5TH MARCH 2019 FROM BARBADOS ROTARY CLUB:

You are very welcome. Thank you for reaching out to us back in December. We were happy to play a small role in Dawn's mission and we look forward to maintaining the link between Dawn, you and family as we all do our part to reduce the use of single use plastics and the pollution they bring to our oceans.

 As you cope with the mild English temperatures, I hope you will find some warmth in the memories and friendships created on your short visit to Barbados. Please stay in touch

Thank you

To my sponsors and 250 club members

Green Recycling

Station Automotive,

Stansted Airport MAG, Chronicle systems, SEAGO, Hillside Playcare, The Rose Inn, Burnham Yacht Harbour, The Old Salt Loft,

Winter and Co, Clear Thinking I, Travel Map, ROK Electricals, Royal Burnham Yacht Club, Art Pakk, Simply Stoves, Fantastic less Plastic, Blackwater (Band) Barry & Sheila Smith, Jaime Wood, Gary and Zoë, Cath de Vincentiis, Charlie Pitcher, Kiko Matthews, Sheila Clarke, Kimberley Ann, Steve Sidaway, Robin & Sonia, Chris Neal, Chelmsford RFU, Burnham on Crouch Coastal Rowing Club, Jo-Ann Greene, Mick Rosier, Essex Police Sports Association, Angela and Alex G, PACT For Autism, Rowhedge Coastal Rowing Club, Creeksea Sailing Club, Chickens and Dogs, Amelia & Laila, Vanessa Bell, David and Glenys Hopkin, 2531 Gang, Happy Hearts, Brightlingsea Coastal Rowing Club, Benedict Clarke, SWFYC Rowing Section, Mike Lewis & Di Bailey, WLDF (Women's Leadership Development Forum), Bev's Bucket, Jean Taylor, Steve & Pam, Mary-Ann Munford, Burnham on Crouch Fire Station, The Frederick Leistikow Lodge, Mitre Lodge, Lodge of St Peter, Heidi and Jim Gibson, Thomas Hart SNR, Burnham on Crouch Carnival Committee, SWF Inner Wheel, Essex Police PPU, Mini and Rob, St Josephs and St Francis, The Brownes, Elsbeth Cowell, Caz Becker

Jaime Wood. Barry & Sheila. Gary & Zoe. Sheila Clarke. Mary-Ann Munford. Kiko Matthews. Kimberly Ann. Steve Siddway. Robin & Sonia. Chris Neal. Jo-Ann Greene. Mick Rosier. Angela & Alex G. Amelia & Laila. Vanessa Bell. David & Glenys. Benidict Clarke. Cath De Vincentiis. Charlie Pitcher. Mike Lewis & Di Bailey. Jean Taylor. Steve & Pam. Thomas Hart Snr. Mini & Rob. The Brownes. Essex Police PPU. Caz Becker. Elsbeth Cowell International Financial Data Services

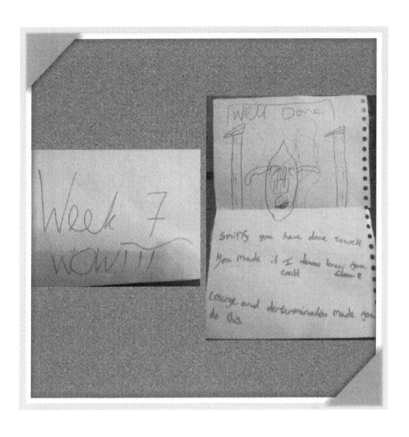

Printed in Poland
by Amazon Fulfillment
Poland Sp. z o.o., Wrocław